Discover Your S

"The processes Kathryn Hudson offers in *Discover Your Soul Mission* are life-changing as they guide us step-by-step into a deeper, richer, more colorful way of living. By reading this book you will never feel alone again, and you will know how to tap into the angelic and universal resources and wisdom you deserve and thrive in this new time for humanity."

~ **LILOU MACÉ,** webTV interviewer, video blogger, and author of *The Yoni Egg*

"*Discover Your Soul Mission* is a hands-on, step-by-step guide helping you to penetrate the layers the world has placed over your individual light to find your own sweet spot and flow. As always, Hudson's tone is light and easy, a gentle voyage to the soul. Read it and find your shine!"

~ **KATHY TYLER,** coach and co-creator of *The Transformation Game*, *The Original Angel Cards*, and Frameworks for Change®

"Kathryn Hudson's new book, *Discover Your Soul Mission,* brings another pearl to the treasure she has been sharing with her followers in the United States and abroad. In it, she adds a spiritual and even biblical dimension to the conversation about the meaning of life, bringing angels and the 'seeding' of our being (God forming each and all while still in the womb) with our unique 'sweet spot' (our God-given gifts freely bestowed upon us), for us then to offer out into the world by simply following our sweet spot of joy. As ever, an excellent read, with Hudson's humor and conversational style rendering deep material light and even fun to read, with excellent exercises to get to know our individual sweet spots better. Highly recommended."

~ **REV. EVERETT THOMAS, Ph.D.,** rector, St. Francis by the Sea

"Kathryn Hudson really is an angel guiding us to reconnect with who we truly are. Her *Discover Your Soul Mission* is a playful and deeply insightful book that supports us in our daily life and helps us find our true mission here on Earth. Sometimes you laugh out loud and sometimes you shed a tear—her wonderful stories and teachings are profound messages that we need to read again and again. I highly recommend Kathryn's new book, such a delight and written in such a light and clear way."

~ **FRANS STIENE,** cofounder of the International House of Reiki and author of *The Way of Reiki, The Inner Heart of Reiki,* and *Reiki Insights*

DISCOVER *Your* SOUL MISSION

Calling on Angels to Manifest Your Life Purpose

Kathryn Hudson

FINDHORN PRESS

Findhorn Press
One Park Street
Rochester, Vermont 05767
www.findhornpress.com

Text stock is SFI certified

Findhorn Press is a division of Inner Traditions International

Disclaimer
The information in this book is given in good faith and intended for information
only. Neither author nor publisher can be held liable by any person for any loss
or damage whatsoever which may arise from the use of this book or any of the
information therein.

Cataloging-in-Publication data for this title
is available from the Library of Congress

ISBN 978-1-64411-523-7 (print)
ISBN 978-1-64411-524-4 (ebook)

Printed and bound in the United States by Lake Book Manufacturing, Inc.
The text stock is SFI certified. The Sustainable Forestry Initiative® program
promotes sustainable forest management.

10 9 8 7 6 5 4 3 2 1

Edited by Nicky Leach
Text design and layout by Anna-Kristina Larsson
This book was typeset in Garamond, Spartan and Magneta Condensed

To send correspondence to the author of this book, mail a first-class letter
to the author c/o Inner Traditions • Bear & Company, One Park Street,
Rochester, VT 05767, USA and we will forward the communication,
or contact the author directly at **www.kathrynhudson.net**.

CONTENTS

PART ONE

The Voyage Out—Forgetting

PART TWO

Recognizing the Call of Your Soul—
The Re-membering

Preface
LEAVING THE BLANKET FORT

*H*ey, God's Light! Yeah, you! Are you ready to leave that blanket fort to come out and play?

But maybe I am getting ahead of myself here.

I woke up this morning to air that is surprisingly cool, with the sun peeking out from behind the building across the way and into my window here in Paris. The combination made the morning feel clean, somehow, crisp and shiny, and made me want to leap from my bed to begin writing.

Then, very quickly, an equal and opposite feeling came along: my feet were cold. So instead of leaping up from the bed and closing the half-open window to get on with the writing that was tapping at my brain, I burrowed farther under the covers, making of my very soft blanket a kind of fort: a soft stronghold inside of which I was protected against the cold dangers of the world. But of course, unfortunately, that "protected" me against my writing, as well.

Of course (as I am writing to you now), with determination, I got out of that blanket fort pretty quickly, thereafter, not allowing the part of me that wanted to say no to this day, that wanted to hide under the sweet sweet covers of my blanket fort, to win. Since I could see exactly what was going on, I chose to say, "Yes, yes, oh, hell, yes!" to a day of creativity, of wonder and growth, feeding the hiding part of me instead.

The dynamic is one that is perhaps familiar. Any comfort zone in which we find ourself is like that bed: cozy, if a bit stifling. And unknown territories, such as a new day, a new job or relationship, a new book, or well, anything *new*, can seem possibly exciting but also maybe a bit terrifying, so we may be enticed to stay put under cozy covers.

The problem with a comfort zone that demands that we say no to the new when it comes calling is that nothing can grow there but inertia. The "new" that beckons us is connected to the emerging part of our being, and our aligning with our soul mission, so yes, it can be scary as well as tempting, prompting perhaps both an "Eek!" and a "Yay!," a phenomenon that I (with great creativity) call the "eek-yays"; in other words, situations in which we are both intrigued and excited for something new to be born into our lives, and terrified of letting go of what we need to release in order to live at that next level.

We will discuss what those marker feelings denote, and how to navigate the eeks and the yays, the no's and yes's, safely and pleasurably in the company of Angels in this book.

Suffice it for now to say that it is the yes and the no within us that we will explore here, knowing that our yes brings us to growth (in alignment with our soul's purpose in being here—yay!) and that the no is the fear of the unknown, programmed into us since birth (eek!). This last will always try to keep us from growth, distracting and dissuading us from the next-level life that is calling to us. Saying yes to coming out from under the covers, to stretching in the direction of our light and soul's mission, is a grand task, one perhaps most easily achieved with a little help from some friends in high places: the Angels and our soul. In this book, we will open to that assistance.

If you are reading this, your soul is calling!

I always get a chuckle when I hear people say that they are trying to "find themselves." In an age when overconsumption and materialism is increasingly resulting in disenchantment with that way of being, we see that a thirst and search for depth and meaning is ever more ubiquitous. On my own path, I meet and accompany many who are awakening to their desire to play the game of life differently, looking for fulfillment within and aligning their living and working with that. The fact that this phenomenon is on the rise is very good news; it augurs well for humanity, and the earth as a whole.

But there is even better news.

Your soul is calling you now, and when your soul is calling you, unless you keep your eyes and ears and, well, whole body squeezed tightly shut under the covers, you cannot miss it! There are no accidents, no "coincidences," and if you are reading this book, you may already be "hearing" (or seeing or feeling or knowing) that call. In this book, we will open to our unique ways of knowing, our spiritual gifts, which guide us along the path.

When someone dies with regrets at the end of life, it is certain that they have missed all or part of their soul mission. This book is about not missing, about *finding*, that meaning, that purpose. It is dedicated to rendering clear what the name of the game is, what our soul's purpose is, and how we can step into action in alignment with that purpose—with the help of divine guidance from the Angels, and from our soul!

For this reason, this book is dedicated to my soul, which brought me (kicking and screaming, sometimes) to this page, this time, this meaning, in order to share the Joy of this reunion, this conscious realignment, with you, my readers!

The book is also dedicated to the Angels, particularly the Guardian Presence and the Archangels, which support this reunion, the band getting back together, the conscious reunion of our human aspect (the instrument) with our sacred soul (the musician), and the Angelic team (booking agents) assembled since before you were born!

Your soul is calling you, right now, and has been for a long time—your whole life, actually.

Every time you meet someone for the first time but feel like you have known them forever (you have), your soul is calling you, reminding you of truth. Every time you explore a new city, or neighborhood, yet somehow find yourself on familiar terrain, your soul is calling you. Any time your eyes fill with tears upon hearing a melody, anthem, hymn, or song, your soul is calling you, reminding you, poking at you under the covers.

These moments pierce the structures of this world and the rules of the game to trigger a memory of that which has (for most of us) been forgotten. These are instances out of time and space where we Re-member, where our physical being is suddenly synced with our spirit-being, our soul. Such moments are sacred, and our bodies recognize them (even if our head doesn't, or doesn't care to) with tears or goosebumps maybe, or flushing, heat, or chills. The body knows when the soul is about.

So, finally, this book is dedicated to all who seek—that they may (as ever) find; and to all who are hiding under the covers, fearful—that they might relax and find peace and the confidence to emerge. After all, your soul's got this, and the Angels are ready to assist!

If you feel like something is missing, if you have been seeking, or even thinking about seeking, if you are reading this book, your soul has called you here. The alarm has sounded. It is time to head out from the blanket fort into the world to play. Your role awaits. You've got this! You are ready!

But don't just take my word for it, even though this book will bring you along, step by step. It is your heart—that inner GPS we all have that we can trust with our lives, literally!—that will know your readiness as you play with the chapters that follow.

Yes, play! The highest and best of humanity expresses itself in the heart and breeds Joy. The age of martyrs has passed. All souls active today, all of us, are fed by Joy, the yes to each day and to each way that supercedes any stinkin' thinkin' no.

So don't forget to have fun!

A RECOMMENDATION, AND A NOTE OF THANKS

*I*f you have read any of my work up to this point, you already know that I was graced by a visitation: An Angel walked into the bank where I was working, in the middle of Manhattan in New York City, to give me a wakeup call and with it, an amethyst crystal reminder.

So while you absolutely do not have to believe in Angels or call on them to help with your journey of discovery of *your* soul mission, I highly recommend it! The path will flow more smoothly, with more lightness and ease, if you welcome the help of your Angels. For this reason, the exercises in this book include opening up to Angels for assistance: it just makes sense. That said, the personal excavation and discovery exercises to be found herein can also be done without angelic assistance: you are pretty powerful, too!

Here, at this moment on the path, I dedicate this book with a thankful heart to the Angels who have helped me, who have been so clearly present and rendered the path more joyful, and the writing of this book more filled with Light.

Part One

THE VOYAGE OUT—
FORGETTING

Chapter 1

COURAGEOUS SOUL—
LIGHTWORKERS AND
BEINGS OF LIGHT

*H*ey, God's Light! Yeah, I'm talkin' to you! Who else would I be talking to? Of course, I could be talking to anybody, but right now, here, at this moment, only you and I and the Angels are present.

But I am getting ahead of myself.

The goal of this book is to have fun while we clarify what our soul mission is—to find our life purpose—and why not with Angelic assistance? Then, we will have the chance to put in place a distinct plan to effect the transformation of our life in such a way as to feel the fulfillment of our purpose, even as we go through our lives each day. To achieve that end, we'll start at the beginning. To steal from the Bible, in the beginning, God said, "Let there be light." And so, there was you!

But before we get down to the more analytical work we will get up to here together, let's begin with some definitions so we have a common ground of discussion going forward.

I called you "God's Light," and I meant it.

From a spiritual perspective, each being on Earth is an expression of God (or the Universe, Love, Creation—insert the word that suits you here), as *there is no place that God is not*. Animals, plants, trees, seas, and you all express purely that highest light of God. Humans express it in ways that are a bit more complicated, true—a function of the uniquely human free will; however, we all express the light of creation (in some, more easily recognized than others, admittedly) in our own quite unique way.

From a scientific perspective (and isn't living in a time when science and spirituality are aligning so very exciting?), everything that exists, including us, is made of light in waves/particles. We now know that even things that seem very solid (pinch me!) are made of light. They tell us that there is much more empty space in our bodies, in every cell of every body, than there is matter.

Why does this matter? It matters because our consciousness is evolving.

In the past, the nature of matter was thought to be simple: solid, gas, and liquid were the only three states of matter. Now, we know better. Waves and particles and other in-between states are being recognized all the time, and what was imagined to be cut and dried is, well, not!

This is cutting-edge, frontier stuff. Gratitude to the scientists who were the first to dare to leave the blanket fort of our simplistic understanding of the nature of things, to fling open the doors of understanding, despite having to pass through the resistance of their field, risking ostracization and material security, tracing a path for us all to follow.

It matters that we are not only "matter"; that is, purely physical beings, since this book (why we are here together today) is about aligning with that which is our non-physical aspect, pure Light, our soul, our Divine expression of Source. This work is all about recognizing why we are here, and getting down to consciously accepting a mission that we both chose and didn't choose, as beings of both Light and matter. Our intangible soul chose the mission, and our human consciousness did not.

Huh?

Let me begin at the beginning. As with everything I teach, I invite you to consider what is set out here, to question it, and to feel intuitively if it resonates for you. Your inner heart is the perfect compass to navigate life's voyage. Use it to notice if this feels true for you.

Here on Earth, we operate in space and time. Things seem simple, linear, and tangible, but before we were here, we were there.

"There," meaning at Source, is whence we came, and where we all head to back after our voyage here (this life) is complete. The unity of God in all things, sometimes called Trinity, transcends duality. It is what we might imagine as the ultimate blanket fort, combining the safety of what is comforting and the excitement of creative space. It is ideal for new voyages, first imagined and then experienced.

Each soul (and we've all got 'em!) is an expression of that Source, like a wave is an expression of the ocean. Like that wave emerging for a time from the ocean, we emerge from Source for a time, our soul evolving through lifetime expressions. When our "wave," or life journey, is complete (aka death), we recede, returning to the eternal blanket fort of Source until the soul's next expression, next journey, next game, is revealed.

As such, each life is specifically directed by Source through our soul into the earth plane (or elsewhere) to have a specific experience, live a specific movement, experience a specific evolutionary voyage that can be called our soul's mission.

Every soul has one. Many souls have more than one. The "why," or mission, of life can be very clear (as in the case of one with a distinct artistic or athletic prowess, a prodigy born with certain capacities), or decidedly unclear (people who feel like they are lost or somehow like they haven't found their meaning, those for whom the voyage seems to be missing something. This book is especially for that second group, the one to which I myself once belonged, until I found my way, my sweet spot.

When we are ready to come out of our human-made blanket forts, it is most often because our comfort zone can become quite stifling. We may yearn to venture out into the world to renew our excitement for life, our life force, our vitality, even if we are afraid to do so.

When a wave emerges and expresses its "waveness," it, too, seizes an opportunity to express energy in its own unique way. For a wave it is simpler, of course—up and down, one time. For us, well, let's just say there is decidedly more than one up and down in our lives. It might be more accurate to say that we emerge and then play, both beneath and atop the covers, until finally, we go back under the "covers" of unconditional love and safety, the divine blanket fort.

When our soul is ready to emerge, we co-create with Source (God) the plan for our lifetime voyage. We decide what our mission is, or what our missions are, and then the choice of "role"—the human form we choose to help us undertake our goals—is put into place to optimize the chances of completion of our mission, despite the difficulties of the earthly terrain. We choose the context of life that will allow for the best chances of the fullness of the evolutionary expression of our individual waves of mission.

Let's look at some examples of possible soul missions to get a clearer idea of this concept.

Souls That Express as Non-Physical Beings of Light

A soul might choose to emerge to take on a voyage that is simpler and more natural, especially if the preceding experience/lifetime was a rough one—imagine small, peaceful waves coming after stormy ones. For example, the chosen mission might be a pure contribution of Light to the Universe, and the soul might choose to take on the role of a Being of Light, not on Earth but elsewhere; as part of the Pleiades, perhaps.

Similarly, the soul might choose a voyage/expression as a guide on the other side of the veil, opting perhaps to support and accompany another soul expressing as a human on Earth—an erstwhile friend or family member, perhaps, or an artistic prodigy, in the case of a soul that has already integrated a high expression of that prodigy's work—imagine Shakespeare, Merlin, or Beethoven guiding a writer, a healer, or a composer, for example.

If an advanced soul wants to assist with Earth's particular evolutionary challenges at this time without getting stuck in the concrete, so to speak, it might choose a life as an elemental being, breathing life into trees, plants, and flowers, for example, and whispering guidance and support for any humans who know how to listen.

Each of these are Beings of Light, easily understood as such, but the souls who take on physical form are no less expressions of God's Light and Love. Let's look at some of these.

Souls That Express as Animals

An advanced soul might incarnate as an animal on Earth, but that option entails a choice: Will the soul take on the form of a wild animal, a domestic one, or even an animal that will be mistreated by humans?

An animal in the wild expresses pure frequency, and is an elemental force uplifting the general frequency of the planet (which is why extinctions are bad news, creating serious planetary imbalance). These days, such souls are helping to call attention to and wake up humanity to such imbalances.

Or the soul might choose to come in as a pet or domestic companion, ready to help their humans evolve on their path, as expressions of pure love (like a dog), or as a familiar (perhaps a cat), ready to guide the humans they accompany (if the human knows how to listen). No animal comes into our home by accident. These are always soul contracts, and the free will of the human either permits or does not permit the evolution that the contract was set up to allow. We will talk more about soul contracts later.

Finally, a very advanced soul might even choose an incarnation as an animal that is abused or ill treated by humans in an effort to awaken humans by shock effect. This is why humankind's general exploitation of and extreme cruelty to animals is now awakening in many sensitive humans the urge to rectify the situation; this is the impulse behind animal rights movements and vegetarian/vegan dietary shifts. It is important to note that, in this extreme case, as in all cases, the soul (of the animal and of the human) is perfectly fine, always whole and always eternal. Such creatures are animated by great souls undertaking difficult tasks voluntarily to awaken humanity and assist earthly evolution.

A Word about Earth's Evolution

As we look at soul purpose, we should be aware that every soul that incarnates on Earth chooses a mission that, if brought to fruition, will contribute to the evolutionary path of the earth. What does this mean?

For millennia, the earth has been weighed down, imprisoned in the clutches of fear. Humans, in particular, are both subjected to and contribute to that fear, and sometimes infect animals with it. Every fearful thought that has ever been thought or expressed aloud is, in alignment with the Law of Conservation of Matter and Energy you may have learnt about at school, still in existence. In this, we are truly creators! As a result, the earth is covered by an energetic cloud of fear.

You will have noticed that fear (and its expressions: worry and stress) is often expressed by those around us, maybe even by us, but the truth of who we are is that we are Beings of Light, expressions of Source. As such, we are always truly safe at home eternally (out of time and space) with God. So our highest expression is to express love, not fear. Fear (not hate) is the opposite of Love; hate is simply a violent expression of fear.

We known this to be true, don't we? Kids come in with hearts full of love, until they learn otherwise, right?

We all come into this world ready to love. Children don't see color or class. These petty and illusory (from an eternal perspective) distinctions are learned and then encrusted in habit. Even in our families, we start off as small children with hearts wide open and full of hope, but then (even in the best of families), as our love and attention cannot always be met, 24/7, with reciprocal love and attention, we learn to minimize our expectations.

At some point, we take a step back and hide our love so as not to be hurt. In the beginning, human interactions in the family or at school and later with friends, colleagues or lovers often will harden into habit our fear of expressing our love openly and easily. We learn to hold our breath unconsciously, as fear of what will happen next blocks us from allowing our love to flow naturally into our highest expression of soul and Light.

As such, the current evolutionary path of our planet is the story of human evolution. We are the reason that love is not the all-embracing atmosphere on Earth. For the most part, unconsciously and instinctively, we have closed our hearts off, protecting ourselves either entirely or partially, opening only to certain people in certain situations. This situation explains why so many people are drawn to animals, as they are a safe expression of love, and allow some of us to express that which wants most to be expressed within and through us: pure love.

In releasing the fear that led us to close our hearts, the earth (of which we are part) evolves, one opening heart at a time; each person unburdened from the pressure of fear and its accompanying repression of Love and Joy unburdens the earth.

Souls That Express as Humans

We have already seen that a soul can express as a pure Being of Light or it can incarnate and take on a more challenging physical form.

But if a soul wishes to take on an even greater challenge, it might choose to incarnate as a human on Earth, a context where duality exists within space and time, where the light of Source seems split into light and darkness, love and fear! The brave soul might choose to take on a human body born to a human family and culture, knowing full well the likelihood of getting lost in the forgetting that a human incarnation entails.

But, as we saw with the many choices available to a soul choosing an animal lifetime, the hardy soul who chooses to incarnate as a human also has choices.

New Soul, Baby Steps

A new soul—that is, a soul recently emerged from Source with few if any foundational lifetimes behind it—will most often choose a life that will allow them to dip their toes in the earthly water with a simple purpose: experiencing the materiality the physicality of existence, or, as one goes on, perhaps experiencing love, or generosity, learning to share, learning to communicate, for example. (**Note:** each of these simple missions can also be undertaken by a more evolved soul in greater depth in a given lifetime.)

These lifetimes represent a steep learning curve, and though the lifetime/context may sometimes seem "simple," the human expression of the soul will not find these lifetimes simple. This human might live life a bit like a bull in a china shop, creating a mess around them. Earth is not the easiest of training grounds.

More Advanced Soul, Karma Steps

A new soul like the one described above will create karma for itself, and in later lifetimes will choose to balance that karma to evolve, to be released from the yoke it represents.

A Word about Karma

As a soul is evolving, lifetime after lifetime, karma may be incurred, experienced as weight, and then released by a balancing action. The resistance of that weight brings the soul into growth, realigning to Source, step by step.

If we think again about waves, imagine that a wave's movement toward the shore is always met with an equal movement from that shore. In all things, there is balance. In this we see another underlying Law of Energy: In all that is, energy seeks equilibrium.

So if in a previous lifetime, a soul expressed as a human who did harm to others, that soul might choose to express again as a human, but this time as one who will experience harm or one who abhors harm and works against all harm to others in the current lifetime. Equally, one who stole might be stolen from, or might protect others from theft; one who hated might be hated or stand in mediation to quell hatred; or one who craved and perhaps tasted great success might choose to taste its opposite and be humbled by earthly "failure."

That last example might be surprising to you, as here on Earth we consider earthly success "good" and earthly failure "bad," but remember that the truth of the soul is that we are eternal and safe in God always (the divine blanket fort). Each outing/voyage/lifetime permits the soul to evolve and advance, and the experiences in the individual lifetimes are only put in place to permit that. What happens in Vegas—or anywhere else, for that matter—stays (literally) in Vegas, on Earth. When we realign with soul and Source, only the richness of the experience and the evolutionary impact it brings is preserved.

When a soul has evolved and realigned with Source completely, it steps out of karma, as opposites align in unity, in oneness. That said, if you are reading this book (and for me, the one writing it), we are most likely not at that point just yet!

Souls That Express Beauty and Extreme Talent

Like the Light Beings noted above, certain humans are conceived of and created to allow the soul to express pure beauty in creation. These are, of course, the rare pearls of humanity who create masterpieces of music, art, or literature or express the ideal in sport or form that inspires others to reach for more, to express higher frequencies.

Such humans are often single-minded, entirely engrossed by their passion. As such, sometimes they are not the easiest people to be around and can seem selfish or narcissistic. That dichotomy of Light and Dark can only express in the duality of the earthly plane, and shows clearly that the soul concerned is not necessarily what we like to call "advanced." Such human imperfection, though, is often planned. This can allow the humans around such beings to feel compassion for them, not engulfed or overwhelmed by the perfection of their work.

Souls That Express in Disability, Sickness, and Hardship

While the souls of the last section that express high talent and beauty in human form are esteemed and deemed "successful" by the world, on the other end of the spectrum of human perception are the souls that express as humans who are regarded as being burdened with disabilities or undergoing various hardships.

Though the world does not hold such beings in high esteem, these are perhaps the most challenging of all missions, and are only undertaken by very advanced souls. These souls choose a life path that is difficult in human terms, but which can evoke in other human hearts an awakening of selflessness, such as compassion and generosity.

Such human beings can be said to present no threat to another human being, either through their extreme disability or poverty, and so, in a context with no threat, other humans' capacity to be loved is released. Such souls make us better for their presence around us. The world may deem them weak, but they are, in fact, the souls that shine brightest and inspire others to shine as well. (Remembering a little boy then young man named Danny, along with many others here.)

Souls That Express Briefly as Humans and Die Very Young

A soul that dies very young, either in the uterus or as a baby, has a specific mission, always in the context of a soul contract. Even if accidental, such deaths are no accident. No death or end of voyage occurs without the soul (and its highest expression, God) being in agreement. The brevity of an existence does not at all limit its impact (just as a person can live a long life with little impact); it is all about soul intention. The soul form that resulted in miscarriage or early death most often stays connected to its human mother or parents and will often serve as a guide for them. The departure of such a soul will somehow be of service to the lives of those left behind.

It is important to note also that a soul whose physical form is terminated intentionally also creates a powerful movement in the person who chose the termination, as well as all those impacted by it. This choice, often made from a place of fear, invites a healing and balancing through forgiveness and love.

These briefly expressing souls may undertake such missions for the purpose of karmic balancing for themselves or to accompany family members as part of what is often called a "soul contract."

A Word about Soul Contracts

A soul contract is set up by two or more souls before their birth (outside of space and time), as a decision to work together at some point on their paths, a deal meant to create an opportunity for growth for both or all parties.

The soul contracts in our lives are easily recognizable when we look for them. They are the experiences, positive or negative, that mark us the most. They can be denoted by positive influencers in our lives, such as the person who teaches us how to express our passion to write or sing, or they can be marked by negative influencers, such as the person who turned an addict onto drugs, or the abuser's impact on a child, leading them to mistrust people.

Whether we experience them in a way we call "positive" or "negative," the soul contracts we experience in our lives are always positive on the eternal level; that is, they occur in order to optimize the possibility of achieving and fully expressing our soul's mission in this lifetime.

While from our human perspective the planet is in duality, from the higher perspective of soul, Source, or eternity, all is oneness; everything is moving in and out, to and from center. No matter what occurs on Earth, it does not disturb the perfect harmony that lies beyond the veil in nondual reality of the unity of Source. As such, even nightmarish experiences can be imagined to have their place in the rhythm of the movement of Source through duality.

A metaphor might help. Imagine a loving parent watching their child sleeping and noticing that the child is struggling in their sleep, obviously having a nightmare. While the parent, from a place of compassion, may want to wake the child from the nightmare, they know with certainty that even if the experience is not pleasant, the child is safe. Similarly, from the eternal perspective, like a good parent, Source is always aware of us and sees and knows that our soul—the truth of who we are—is always safe.

They say, rightly, that all earthly experiences are either a cry for love or an invitation to love; as such, all situations that mark us give us reason to stretch toward the expression of God's Love that we are. Even when we shut down and close our hearts, that movement will impel the opposite movement, the opening to follow—if we allow it. (Later on, we will discuss allowing or not; that is, free will.)

Advanced Souls That Express as Lightworkers

Another way that advanced souls express in humankind is as Lightworkers, the sector of humanity that is here specifically to assist, more and more consciously, in humanity's (and the earth's) evolution. If you are reading this book, it is likely that you are one such soul. But let's check!

How can you know if you are a Lightworker? Here are some tell-tale signs that might ring familiar to you:

1 A Lightworker has **a sense of mission or purpose**. They might not always know what their purpose is, but they have a deep and clear inner knowing that they have one. This sometimes is expressed inversely as a strong sense of *not* being where they are meant to be, or *not* doing what they are meant to be doing (which proves that there is rhyme and reason to their existence; they just haven't found it yet). If this is the case for you, you're in the right place. This book is a path to finding that "sweet spot" where you know you are where you are meant to be, doing what you are meant to be doing. Not all humans feel this sense of purpose, though all souls do have a purpose in incarnating; however, not all who have a sense of purpose are Lightworkers, so let's continue.

2 A Lightworker is very **sensitive** and has a strong sense of the invisible sacred, which (to most of humanity) does not exist. Their **gifts of clairvoyance** (intuition, clairaudience, clairvoyance, clairsentience) are at least somewhat open. We will speak of these gifts later on.

3 A Lightworker will have had at least some **sacred experience** that marked them in the past: seeing, hearing, feeling, or simply being aware of an invisible presence around them (either "negative" or "positive"). But again, not only Lightworkers have clairvoyant gifts, so let's continue.

4 A Lightworker will, on a human level, feel **called to service**. These folks will have always been helpful, even as a child. These givers sadly often don't know how to receive, but they will continue always to give. (We will talk about finding balance in this giving and receiving later on.)

5 **If you are reading this right now**, it is highly likely that you are a Lightworker. Just sayin'.

Angelic Assistance—What, How, and Why?

What Is Angelic Assistance?

Although a Lightworker is an evolved soul with plenty of powerful potential, and can realize the soul mission on their own, fortunately, even a Lightworker doesn't have to go it alone. At the moment that the choice for a lifetime is made, God or Source commits to accompany us during each lifetime—we are not just dropped off in duality, far from "home," and abandoned. This Guardian Presence of God (expressed as our Guardian Angel) emerges to accompany each stalwart soul that chooses the challenge of an earthly life, with the sole/soul purpose of accompanying the soul in its human form and supporting the chosen mission.

In addition to the angelic entourage of Guardian Presence, which is with us from before we are born, humans can also call on *Archangels* to access particular Divine qualities when we most need them.

How Can We Access Angelic Assistance?

Sometimes, as with what happened to me, the Angels will facilitate this and come to us. They might do something to catch our attention (maybe with a rock), nudging us in the direction of our soul and our mission. Normally, Angels, even our Guardian Angels, cannot intervene in our lives without our invitation, but our invitation can be simply in the form of an "Oh dear, God, help me!" As Angels are not separate from, but an expression of, God or Source, they reply readily; in fact, they await your cue, as they are bound to respect your free will during this time you pass here on Earth. Of course, a direct invitation of "Please, Angels, step forward and assist" will also work nicely, or any other such words. Your words, spoken from the heart, are always the best, and the Angels will read the intention of your heart.

Generally, as above, we access angelic assistance by calling on them, directly or indirectly, by calling on God or the Divine under any name. The angelic realm will always wait for our invitation, out of respect for the *free will* granted to humanity in order to allow the soul to grow and evolve through earthly experience. We will discuss this free will, and the ramifications of it, later.

The only circumstance in which an Angel can intervene without our express invitation is when the human is facing a situation with risk of death, when it is not yet time; that is, not aligned with the soul plan. No one dies unless the soul is ready for the voyage to end. In such a case, the Angel intervenes with the accord and at the behest of the soul. This is most often part of a soul contract, where the Angel has agreed with the soul that the human would have a near death experience, opening up the possibility of rebirth and change, in alignment with the soul's mission.

As mentioned above, in addition to the Guardian Angels that accompany us, it is also possible to invoke Archangels to assist us. Each Archangel expresses a Divine quality. We can ask the Archangels to bolster us in that quality and to help us find and cultivate those qualities in ourselves and others. We will work with a number of Archangels here later on, specifically related to our soul purpose.

Why Should We Access Angelic Assistance?

In a world that most often teaches us that we need to toughen up, go faster; that if we want something we have to go get it ourselves; that no one is paying attention; and that there is no help for us, the Angels remind us that none of that is true! Calling out for angelic assistance immediately brings magic into the air, and Divine assistance and Love is truly only a call away. This is an echo of the eternal truth of who you are. Don't believe me? Try it!

With Angels or without Them? The Choice Is Yours!

The truth is, as proposed in my last book, we do not have to "go it alone" here. And if you are reading this, you may already know this: There is help. We are powerful beings, and we can step into that power and live fully our mission without help, but why go that route? Why not accept help? Why not accept and cultivate the relationship with the Divine that will render every step sacred and every passage clearer?

The choice, of course, is yours. You can absolutely work through the exercises in this book without asking the Angels for help. I wouldn't, personally. Angels are really fun to be around and can offer powerful insights. But it is your call!

With all that said, what happens after the soul has made its choice and the Guardian Angels are on board? So glad you asked!

Chapter 2

Courageous Human— Ideal Vessels

*U*ntil this point, we have been looking at the soul's purpose from only the prior-to-this-life experience. After each life, the soul is guided by Source to ascertain if its purpose has been fulfilled in that lifetime. If yes, the soul goes on to its next evolutionary step, if it is still evolving; if no, the purpose is carried forward. We are given unlimited opportunities to experience what we have chosen as our mission.

There is only one problem with that: *We* don't choose that mission, do we? Our soul (in conjunction with Source, God) sets/accepts a mission; we humans don't. At least not at the outset! So, it could be said that we have been conscripted (lovingly, but conscripted nonetheless) for a job we are not even aware of! Where is the free will in that?

Before we get our panties in a twist, yes, we do have free will! We have the option to say yay or nay to the mission as it beckons to us in ways that keep popping up, maybe every day. At each fork in the road, we can absolutely go toward the mission set out (of which we are most often unaware, though we may notice coincidences and patterns). Nothing says that we have to go along with the voyage the soul has prepared for us. So free will does exist, which is why so many humans die regretful . . .

In fact, our human free will is an important part of the Game of Life here on Earth. Part of the careful preparation on the part of God/our Angels, with soul in co-creation, is the choosing of the vessel, the human form most likely to succeed, the form most apt to choose to align with the plan.

Each of us is carefully conceived of, created, and chosen to optimize the chances of success for our soul mission. Everything comes into play in the choosing: where we are born, to which family, which culture, which economic context, race, language, gender, as well as our individual gifts— what we call our strengths and weaknesses—*all of it* comes into play as the soul chooses a vessel, as God once again blows the spirit of Life into a human form.

But once we are born? All bets are off! This, mainly due to what I call The Forgetting.

The Forgetting

Being born into the duality of the earth necessitates forgetting, and in this space-time place, the unity that is quite apparent at the soul level is deliberately obfuscated, and instead, things seem separate and dualistic: good/bad, rich/poor, male/female, you/me, us/them . . . you get the idea!

While, thankfully, some of these separations are now becoming blurred with human evolution, many are entrenched, and we can easily see how the "isms" stem from this: racism, misogynism, elitism, snobbism, etcetera. Behaviors such as these are learned and exist only on Earth. We are not born with them; they are habits we have picked up along the way. We learn them from the groups that surround us from the beginning: family, of course, but also friends, teachers, schoolmates. This is why the soul's choice of vessel—of us!—is so very important, including into what social context we are born.

Almost all of us forget who we are at the soul level very early on in our journey; the "voyage out" depends on it. Why? Well, close your eyes and imagine the most difficult times of your life; the earliest you can recall, perhaps, but the most difficult. See, feel, know what it was like for you back then. *Ugh,* right? Makes you want to climb back under the covers, maybe?

Now close your eyes, and use your imagination to dream of what it might have been like before you were born into the density here on Earth— Light, unconditional Love, a Divine security blanket fort of beauty and ease. *Ahhhhhh!*

Got it? If we maintained a clear memory of what preceded our emerging into this life, how tempted would we be to jump ship? To quit the game when it got too hard, especially knowing that none of this is real, as only the eternal is real?

It is easy to see why The Forgetting is an important part of being born into a life here on Earth. True, some very young children (they say this fades by three years old) seem to recall what it was like before they were born, even past lives, and others maintain access to their Guardian Angels and "imaginary" (not imaginary!) friends. But this fades for almost all of us.

As for those for whom it does not fade, that Re-membering, that gift (or curse) is part of their life path, part of their mission. For the reasons stated above, it makes life more difficult for them, but in other ways, having that special gift can also be a blessing. On the Earth plane, in duality, one can say that everything is both a blessing and a curse. If we can get beyond calling everything either "good" or "bad," we go a long way to healing that separation for ourselves, and by extension, for the planet. It is always a step toward Re-membering.

Let's take time here to explore the vessel that we each are, unique and chosen specifically to support the voyage in time and space of our soul.

What Kind of Vessel Are You? Physical Form

If we take some time to examine the vessel that we are, we can gain some insight into the soul's aim, by imagining why we were chosen.

Imagine that you are going on a long sea journey. What kind of boat would you choose? Maybe one with a bedroom? Or if you were going to compete at the Olympics in white-water racing, would you choose to compete in a cruise ship? Skiff or yacht, kayak or sailboat, if one decides to head out on the waters, there are so many choices! We would always choose the vessel apt for our purpose, *non?*

Yes, of course, we would! And in the same way, our soul, in co-creation with God/Source, chose us!

Let's take a look at how various aspects of our vessels (our human form) might come into play and give us some ideas about how they might be mission-appropriate.

How would you describe yourself? Tall, short, slim, round, strong, weak, and any and all possibilities in between, humans come in many forms! Recognizing that our specific form serves our specific mission, even on the physical level, we can begin to imagine what that mission might be.

In some instances, we can easily imagine how our physical form serves the mission, *non?* Especially for souls who decide to enter the Earth plane to experience physicality, this seems very clear: for example, very tall people early on in life, who are selected and groomed to play basketball, or very big and strong people, who are selected and groomed to play rough sports such as American football or rugby.

Similarly, children built for speed learn this early on and race about, and children who are agile and flexible also catch sight of these natural advantages (in certain contexts) early on. Even children of exceptional beauty might stand out for this physical aspect early on in life. But what of others who are not so obviously blessed with amazing physical traits? How does the physical serve them? Let's take a look.

Vessels That Overcome Impediments with Determination

In some cases, the soul might choose a vessel that has only a modicum of physical prowess but nevertheless, a ton of desire and determination. This optimizes the possibility of an experience of physicality through obstacles overcome. A smaller person with reasonable sports acumen might train zealously and single-mindedly to even surpass those who are larger with greater natural talent! Such a soul not only lives the experience of the physical realm, but also extends a message to all humans that it is indeed possible to overcome what the world states as limits, when we are sufficiently motivated and driven by soul's passion.

These souls also soften the separation, as they—as in the case of a dancer who has not the classical form the world expects—break the molds and limiting beliefs of this world, opening things up, beautifully.

Short People

Often the world thinks that short people automatically are to be excluded from certain service professions. There is even an old song by Randy Newman about it, saying that we (short people) have no reason to live!

Of course, that is tongue in cheek, and the opposite is true. While the world often considers being short a disadvantage, it is easy to imagine why a soul would choose a short human form:

- A short person is better able to get into small places (caves, tunnels, nooks, and crannies), and so is best prepared to be a spelunker, geologist, tunnel worker, and savior if someone gets stuck in such an environment.
- Being short is helpful in certain explorations of physicality, such as gymnastics and physical balance work, where a lower center of gravity is an advantage.

- A soul might choose a shorter form in order to ensure that the vessel is not intimidating and thus easily welcomed and trusted by others.
- Short people have a natural advantage when working with children, as they are immediately more on a level with them.
- Other reasons? Can you imagine? The possibilities are endless!

Tall People

While the world sometimes imagines that the tall people of the world have it good, ask any tall person and they will tell you it is not all hunky-dory. Finding clothes to fit can sometimes be a challenge, and even moving through a world made for shorter people is not always comfortable (especially in older places, such as the structures of Europe or central Philadelphia, where the buildings were built when people were shorter). Think of the advantage of having short legs on a commercial airplane! In addition, it is harder to go unnoticed for a tall person—any, or all, of which might support the soul in its mission!

While we can perhaps now agree that all things have a blessing side, offset by a curse aspect, we can, of course, imagine roles in line with soul missions where being tall is helpful:

- As stated earlier, souls that choose to play sports like basketball in this lifetime have an advantage if they are tall.
- Being tall is also an advantage for a modeling career, for souls who choose to call attention to and thus bring forth beauty into the world.
- Tall people stand out from the crowd, so their souls might have chosen a mission that will be facilitated by that gift (and definitely, also sometimes a curse). Leaders in all fields: government, entertainment, speakers, etcetera, are aided by height, allowing them to stand out in a crowd.
- Tall people are, in some situations, able to be of service to others in unique ways in everyday life, such as simply reaching for something on a high shelf for a shorter person.
- There are many other possibilities. Can you think of some?

Note: It is important to note that both the "blessing" and the "curse" aspects of any of these characteristics wholly serve the soul's purpose, as we will see shortly.

Physically Very Strong People

Although I am sure we can agree that there is a difference between physical strength and personal strength, in this section, we continue our focus on the physical.

Folks who have physical strength are often born with that ability, but also have perhaps cultivated it. These are souls who have chosen either very physical primary roles or very physical secondary or tertiary roles in this lifetime:

- Examples of a strong person's primary role relying on their strength could include anyone who is in the saving sector: firefighters, police, emergency medical personnel, etcetera. (These are often Lightworkers, committed to helping.)
- Examples of other souls choosing a strong form to support their mission in a primary role (but not in a saving sector) include sports figures, lumberjacks, movers, and any physical laborers who rely on their strength in their work. While not typically considered "helpers," they do a job that others cannot do, and so, render service. Often the physicality of this type of work can allow the soul not to get caught up in a mental rat race.
- An example of where the person's strength is more related to secondary or tertiary roles is when the soul chooses a human form who may be guided to work that does not rely on strength but whose passion outside of work does, such as people who enjoy weightlifting as a hobby or volunteer in service sectors in which physical strength is important.

The notion of *primary, secondary, and tertiary roles* is important. Often, the soul will choose to express in multiple ways that evolve as the person's awareness of the soul connection and mission evolves, such as someone choosing to bring Love into the world as a spouse or a parent, and also through their work roles.

Sickly People

At the other end of the spectrum from physically strong people, we have physically weak human forms. Why would a soul make such a choice? We can imagine that it does not make life easy on the person/vessel, so what could be the roles that such a soul has set its sights on for a mission?

- As mentioned earlier, a sick person, especially a very sick one, is nonthreatening, and so can bring out the best, the Light, in others.

- A soul in a human form that is disabled and needs care offers to other souls around it—often in soul contracts—the possibility of being generous and caring, sometimes to offset karma from past lives, or even this one.
- A being whose physicality is minimal can often live a very intense inner life, on a mental or spiritual level, and "carry" others or the earth along with them.

Thin People

As opposed to height and disability, the characteristics of being thin or round are inherited tendencies that can be worked on and, to a degree, transformed. Whether they are considered a strength or a weakness is linked to our cultural context and acceptance of our vessel, and impacts the level of Joy in our life.

Thin people are either naturally so, or they carefully cultivate that thinness (which, in the extreme, can be dangerous). Either way, a thin human form can serve the soul mission in a number of ways:

- A naturally thin person might be the form chosen by a soul whose mission is served by a being that is more physically flexible and agile, able to experience the world more easily on a physical level.
- An unnaturally thin person who is physically weak can, as noted with regard to sickly people, bring out the generous and the helpful in others.
- An extremely or dangerously thin person is sometimes the result of a choice (conscious or unconscious) to be hard on themselves with extreme diet or exercise forced on a body that naturally has other tendencies. When this is the case, a soul may have chosen this experience in order to transform the human experience into self-acceptance and love, adding that energy of transformation to their lineage and to the atmosphere on Earth (which needs it badly). In addition, the soul may be seeking to eventually be able to help and guide other souls to self-love and acceptance.

Round People

A soul that chooses a rounder form may come into the game as a human born into a family where round is the norm and eating a priority, for example, or it can be learned behavior. This can be for any number of reasons, a few of which we list here:

- Fat people, rightly or wrongly are perceived as less threatening, even jolly. This is excellent for a soul whose purpose will be served by having people accept them and their help or guidance easily.
- Heavy-set people, perhaps born into families that use food as an expression for love, might use food as a replacement for love. (We all know about comfort food, right?) Such a soul might have chosen to optimize the possibility of transforming this false nourishment into real love, thus bringing important healing to the planet through the person they have chosen in this lifetime.
- Round people, through the various health problems that result from being overweight, can experience a real transformation, thus feeding the transformational energies currently on the planet—if the human decides to make that change!

Sensitive People

Though one might argue that sensitivity is more a character trait than a physical one, a person's sensitivity is both a function of and contributes to their physical form.

Huh?

Think of someone, maybe yourself, who is very sensitive. For such a person, a world that goes too fast and too hard can be difficult terrain for simply existing, much less completing some unknown, preordained mission. Unless, that is, the soul (with God), which co-created that person, knew exactly what they were doing!

Of course, that is the case. Nothing was left to chance in the preparation of a lifetime.

A sensitive soul experiences that sensitivity through their body: an onslaught of too much stimulation (positive or negative) can send such a person into a tailspin, either sending them to bed and an earthly hideout blanket fort, or other habits/practices/addictions that can be other blanket fort forms: behaviors that soften the blows of this world. This can include all forms of self-anesthesia: drugs, legal or prescribed; alcohol; and too much of anything: TV, Netflix, Facebook, eating, exercising, what have you. When things get tough, the sensitive soul might want to hide!

The overwhelming energies of the world come into the experience of a sensitive through the physical body via the five senses on which we all agree: sight, sound, touch, taste, and smell, as well as through the energy body and our clairvoyant senses (clairaudience, clairvoyance, clairsentience, and claircognizance/intuition).

In overwhelm, that sensitivity will impact the physical being through the nervous system, and continued onslaughts can easily create physical, mental, and/or emotional issues, leading to sickness, burnout, or depression.

With all that said, why in the world (literally) would a soul choose to incarnate as a sensitive human being?

There are a few reasons, all of which point to sensitives being advanced souls here for higher purposes, or Lightworkers:

- A sensitive person is open to energy and the invisible, feeling even that which is not commonly tangible. This is a person more easily able to move into alignment with the invisible soul and consciously align with their soul mission.
- Contrary to what the world sometimes says, a sensitive person is not weak at all. High sensitivity is an indicator that the person has open clairvoyant gifts, ready to be unopened and utilized. Once they learn how to "play their instrument"; that is, take care of their form so that they can maintain harmony and high-level energy. A sensitive is a superhero!
- Once the sensitive learns to play their instrument, they can access guidance, both for themselves and for others, in line with their soul's purpose.
- A sensitive, once confident in their abilities, can cut through the illusion of this world. They can sense truth (and so, lies) and bolster their body so as to no longer experience overwhelm.

From all of the above, it becomes very clear why a soul would choose a life in a sensitive human form, maybe yours?

············•• **Reflect and Ponder** ••···········

What are the specificities of your physical form?
How might they be of service to your soul mission?

As we can see, both the physical form we are born with and the socio-cultural habits we adopt (either by decision or osmosis) that impact our physical form play into the soul's having chosen us. So let's take a look at these other elements that impacted the choice.

Family and Culture

Where we are born, into which family or context, is no accident. I don't know about you, but when I first heard that, I rebelled. After all, life back in an overcrowded sixth-floor walkup in the Bronx, where I walked on eggshells all the time, waiting for the next explosion (or worse), certainly wasn't any choice of mine!

But with time, practice, and meditation, it became clear to me that all of those experiences, finally, served me.

Every aspect of our beginning life, the only part of our life's journey that the soul can control (thanks to free will), is divinely orchestrated, and effective, even if it didn't feel Divine at the time.

Here are a few examples. Can you think of others?

- A soul that has an unpleasant family life as a child might seek solitude in life, favoring a rich inner life over an outer family life.
- Another soul in an unhealthy family context might come away with the burning desire to do better, and to create a loving family context in their lifetimes.
- A soul that rebelled against a life of poverty as a child might find the drive and desire to create another kind of life for themselves expressing God's abundance.
- Another soul in the same poverty context might find inner richness of simple existence, also expressing God's abundance.
- A soul troubled by sexual or other abuse in the family home might choose celibacy, consecrating the physical being only to spiritual pursuits, or might choose to accompany others who were traumatized in the same way.
- Another soul coming out of the same abusive situation might vow to have children and keep them safe, preserving their innocence as long as possible.

Each soul will feel the impulse to heal early context difficulties in alignment with the soul's plan. It then is up to the human to agree or disagree to follow the impulse or to hide from it.

As we see above, in each negative example, there is rich terrain for the positive. A human being who goes through difficult times, especially as a child, is marked by them; these experiences are the soul's choice, not the child's. As such, it becomes compelling to understand why a soul might choose a harsh environment for a child.

Above, we looked at three harsh examples: abuse, poverty, hardship. Here are some others.

Cultural Stereotypes

They say that behind all stereotypes, there is at least a grain of truth. Perhaps this is so; I can only speak to my native culture, the terrain in which I was planted by my soul, which obviously had both a lot of confidence in my capacity to overcome and a wicked sense of humor.

Each of us is born into a culture, or we arrive at one right after birth. In the former case, our family tree can give us clues to the salient values and traits of our situation. Whether we grow up with our birth parents or not, those with whom we do grow up will model the values and habits we breathe in during childhood that impact us, one way or the other, as we grow.

To illustrate this, I will use my own example.

I grew up in the Bronx, surrounded by many cultures but mainly Irish-American families like mine. Many of my friends' parents had, like my maternal grandparents, emigrated from Ireland and found their first apartments in our neighborhood. This impacted me both positively and negatively and positively again.

Let's take a look at this example:

- *Irish people tend to drink.* This stereotype was confirmed all around me as a child, and I saw a lot of adults very drunk back in those days, not very reassuring for a sensitive child (negative). This tendency led me to begin my own drinking at a very young age (negative), which helped me to deal with my emerging sensitivity and clairvoyance (positive). Once I grew out of this particular crutch, I was well equipped to accompany folks who would like to leave addictions behind (positive, and linked to life purpose).

- *Irish people tend to work hard.* This stereotype certainly was my experience as I witnessed families pulling themselves out of immigrant poverty by their bootstraps (positive), but then also not knowing how or when to relax and stop to smell the roses (negative). When it came time, I did the same myself, working my way through the School of Foreign Service at Georgetown (positive) and now working hard at writing and teaching, having learned that I can make my way in the world (positive). The negative here is that some people who grow up in such contexts are so marked by the fear of poverty (lying behind the hard-working nature) that they live in fear of never having enough (negative), and don't enjoy life as they could. Another negative is a judgment about and lack of patience for folks who do not have the same work ethic, as if working hard is a badge of honor. So every positive has hidden negatives and vice versa.

- *Irish people tend to be jealous.* While this is a silly stereotype, and certainly not limited to Irish people, the "joke" growing up was that no one will ever be happy for our good news; only to hear our bad news. Begrudging the good that happens to others by habit and the linked gossip that is rampant (and not just in Irish circles!) are quite negative aspects of the culture in which I grew up. Of course, in noticing and laughing at such bad behaviors, one might choose to go entirely a different route. And as we will see later on, jealousy is not all bad!

- *Stereotypically, they say Irish people tend to be racist.* I am sure that this is not just true of Irish people but of all people. Most of us humans tend naturally toward people who are like us, people who seem similar. We see the world through our own personal lenses, and the lenses our parents gave us. We are born into (not born with) a fear of the unknown, and that includes people from other cultures. Recognizing that we have those lenses, and then breaking them, can only be done consciously.

In sum: A soul will choose such a context, both in order to advance the individual human along the path to soul mission, and also to transform the larger energetic (stereotype) on the Earth plane.

············•• **Reflect and Ponder** ••···········

What traits have you inherited from your cultural context?
What do you value? What might you reject?
What is most important to you in this?
How could this play into a possible purpose to your life?
(We will use this information later.)

Strengths and Weaknesses

Beyond that which is socially inherited, we all have character traits we deem strengths and others we deem weaknesses, but with regard to the soul's mission, none of them are weaknesses; all play to the strength of the mission.

Huh?

In this world, we are in the habit of judging some traits "good" and others "bad," but, as we have seen before, for the soul, this earthly experience is about surpassing the duality; thus, all experiences are enriching. Those experiences during childhood are particularly enriching, of course, as they were of the soul's choosing. This is why, later on, we will delve more deeply into past, child-level experience, in order to work on a plan for future conscious alignment with why we are here, our soul mission. Whatever we might call them, all weaknesses and strengths are strengths in accordance with the soul's plan.

Strengths

These are obvious, *non?* The soul chooses a form that will possess, or be able to cultivate, the strengths necessary to achieve the mission: a person who can write, paint, or sing; a person with a thirst for knowledge in the fields of medicine, plants and trees, or animals; a person who loves children and wants to treat them or teach them or have them; and so on, ad infinitum. Our humanly recognizable strengths are an integral part of the soul's purpose and were planned accordingly.

Our strengths fall generally into two categories: what we are born with and what we cultivate during our time on Earth. But even the latter category is not an accident—the soul plants the longing for a certain type of experience and then opportunity provides it.

Even what we have cultivated after childhood on the terrain here can be traced back to the soul's choosing before we were born. But we all know folks who do not dare follow what has been planted, who do not follow their dream, their heart's desire, don't we?

Whether our strengths are natural and from birth or learned and cultivated, it is only the combination of the soul's planting and our free will choosing that can ensure they be harnessed to fulfill the mission that brought us to this life.

·············• Reflect and Ponder •············

What are your strengths?
What do you love about yourself? (Come on, don't be shy!)
What strengths were you born with?
What strengths have you cultivated through experience?
(Go ahead and write them down; we will use them later.)

Weaknesses

Weaknesses, perhaps, are less obvious—not that we don't see them (the world often teaches us to focus on them more than our strengths), but perhaps less obvious is how what we consider our weaknesses can be strengths, how they can support the expression of our life's purpose. And yet, it is so.

Each of us has been perfectly conceived of and created by God/Source in co-creation with our soul, with every opportunity to fulfill a particular purpose; nothing was left to chance in the preparation of the lifetime. So instead of judging harshly the bits of ourselves we don't like (mostly because society does not value them), maybe we can instead look at them with the knowledge that everything serves, that we are perfect even in our imperfection.

What follows are some imperfections that are fairly common and viewed by society as "negative." Why would a soul include these elements in the human vessel to optimize the chance for success in their mission?

Meekness

Although society does not always respect the meek, the Bible tells us that something more is going on here, as they will "inherit the earth." A soul might choose a human form that incarnates in a context that diminishes confidence and creates meekness for a number of reasons:

- Transforming the root lack of confidence can bring great healing to the planet.
- Accepting quietness, and not being uncomfortable with that trait, transforms meekness into stillness, always a sign of inner strength.
- People with easy access to a quieter side of themselves can, if they so choose, more easily access a rich inner and spiritual life, closely connected to soul and mission.
- People who accept their quiet nature can bring calm to those around them stuck in drama.
- Finally, a person who is deemed meek is not intimidating and can put others at ease simply and easily, earning their trust and confidence.

Vulgarity

Depending on who you talk to, this is either positive or negative. But why would a soul choose the vulgar to express the Divine? A few thoughts:

- A "vulgar" person is considered lowly and uneducated, but vulgarity can be also an artistic choice with widespread appeal.
- A soul that chooses a mundane even vulgar life might be balancing karma.
- A life deemed vulgar by those who consider themselves elite is often richer in authentic human contact.

Too Smart

Sometimes intelligence is not respected or welcomed and can keep a person on the outside. That said, in so many other contexts, intelligence is a great help in a school-intensive early environment and what follows.

Too Dumb

While one may wish they were smarter, or had an easier time in school, a lack of classical intelligence can lead a soul to expressing other kinds of intelligence and gifts more aligned to their purpose.

These are just a few examples of what one might deem weaknesses, and yet we see how they might serve a Soul's mission.

· · · · · · · · · · · · **Reflect and Ponder** · · · · · · · · · · · ·

What are your "weaknesses"?
How might they serve, in the end, your soul purpose?

All that we have discussed: the physical vessel we inhabit, where our "boats" were set into the waters of life, and the cultural contexts that created currents that carried us a long way (or not)—all of it was set up by Source and soul to optimize your chances for success.

Even the current that brought you to this book is one that invites you to flow in the sense of the voyage, but with the consciousness of soul aligning with human free will.

When we swim upstream, life is difficult, and we may even know that we are going in the wrong direction. The exercises in this book are designed to cultivate confidence in that knowing—in our instrument, in our physical body, as well as our mind and certainly our heart, since the seeds of the mission are planted within! But we don't have to do any of this alone. How great is that?

Chapter 3

ANGELIC ASSISTANCE AND THE RE-MEMBERING

*E*arlier, we spoke about the fact that we are truly Beings of Light, Lightworkers maybe, and that, as souls, we consciously choose this life in co-creation with God/Source/Love. Then we talked about "The Forgetting": the fact that, upon arrival here on Earth, just about every one of us forgets who we were and what mission we set for ourselves before we were born.

When we arrive in the physical body here on Earth, almost all memory of the soul that we are truly and our eternal and intimate unity with God is wiped away, and we begin in a context that is rooted in a specific body and a cultural context that limits and conditions our understanding of the world around us.

The Forgetting is the beginning of our human life path that, as a function of our free human will, brings us either closer to or farther from the mission our soul chose (but we have forgotten). Recapturing what has been hidden deep within us to align with our soul and our mission can be called The Remembering, or Re-membering.

In this chapter and beyond, we will focus on how we can expand that understanding, specifically who or what might help us in The Re-membering. But before we talk about Angels, Archangels, and Guides, let's take a deeper look.

A Word about The Re-membering

We saw earlier that in all of life there is an underlying rhythm of expansion and contraction. The amoeba and octopus move in this way, flowers open and then close, trees grow leaves and then lose them, even human activities like businesses open and close, thrive and then contract. One could imagine this to be a reflection of the natural movement of energy in the universe, and one would be right.

Similarly, The Forgetting is followed by The Re-membering. Each of us emerges from Source as soul, and from soul, as the human writing or reading this right now. Then, at the end of our human life, the body falls away, and we return to soul, which is part of Source: we Re-member!

This always happens at death, but sometimes it can happen during our life!

This book is all about Re-membering; that is, realigning consciously: putting the pieces of the puzzle together in order to find what is buried, seeded, deep within us, and then to move in that direction. While our birth (seeming separation from Source) was not a humanly conscious decision, we can consciously Re-member, align, using our free will and our soul as a team to recognize and realize our mission.

When we work with Angels, we optimize the possibility of Re-membering—Re-membering our mission, Re-membering our soul, and Re-membering that we, too, (along with all creation), are part of God, not separate.

Since one of the Universal Laws of Energy states that "Energy seeks equilibrium," when we work with Angels, our frequency rises and we naturally align with our highest soul expression.

In that way, we let the Angels "carry" us on their wings to Re-membering. And once we arrive at that place of Re-membering, the door to living out our mission opens, and that opens other doors, helping others to recall and Re-member, also.

When we remember that we have a purpose (whether or not we know specifically what it might be), there may be an impulsive part of us that wants to spring into action—not a bad thing in itself; life is enticing us to leave the blanket fort and venture out into the world. Great!

But, especially if we are reasonably capable and not used to asking for help, we may make the voyage harder for ourselves by not asking for help. This does not mean that we will definitely not achieve the mission for which we were born, but it does mean that we will definitely have less fun doing so!

So, who you gonna call?

The Angels!

Calling the angelic team assembled around you since before you were born, the Guardian Presence of God, our Guardian Angels, as well as the Archangels, in alignment with our heart's desire (and so, our mission), makes sense doesn't it? In this chapter, we look at *who* to call. Later, we will look at *how* to do so!

Friends in High Places

As we have seen earlier, all of us, each person on Earth, is the vehicle of choice for achieving a specific mission, expressed as a soul, and God's choosing. But as we have seen, when we are born, we succumb to The Forgetting, and we forget all of it: the soul, the mission, and the Angels of God that have committed to supporting the realization of that purpose insofar as the human being, as the result of our free will, chooses to allow.

Once we are aware of this, even if we are not entirely sure we buy it (I was pretty cynical at one point in my life, when I had put a fair distance between myself and my soul mission), it is a good idea to test it out, to ask for help, and (re)open the door to grace through angelic assistance. Please don't take my word for it. Try it—you'll like it!

I do not ask (or want) you to just believe me; rather, I invite you to try it out yourself, give it a shot, give *them* a shot, a chance to show you how loved you are, how accompanied, and how much easier life can be when we let our "friends in high places" step in and help us!

Let's start with who they are, these friends, the Angels.

Guardian Angels

Often I say that my Guardian Angel walked into the bank that day to give me a crystal, or sent that woman to do it. But what does that mean?

For those who have not yet read my last book, *Inviting Angels into Your Life,* let me be clear about the definition: a Guardian Angel is an expression of God that accompanies us during our stay on Earth.

To debunk one common misconception, there is no such thing as a misconception. Every birth has a soul's choosing, God's creation, behind it. There are no accidents, even if the world refers to some births as accidents!

To debunk a second misunderstanding, God does not just drop us off on Earth and abandon us. Though in the density of the Earth plane and through The Forgetting, we can lose sight of this, the Divine is always at hand, ready to assist, if only we would just ask. The form this loving Presence of God takes can be called the Guardian Presence, our Guardian Angels.

It is very interesting to ask for assistance from our Guardian Angels in fulfilling our soul mission, because they were there when the soul mission was set; in fact, they volunteered to come along for the ride! They are enthusiasm (a word that, at its root, means "filled with God") itself when it comes to our mission, yet wait patiently until we are ready to let them help us.

Our Guardian Angels are with us at every moment, at this very moment! And when we call on them, it is not so that they can come to us, but rather, so that *we remember they are here already!* In so focusing, we open ourselves to them; they are already opened to, and in fact waiting for, us.

Our Angels accompany us until the end of our path here on Earth, and while sometimes, there are others that arrive at certain periods of life (like when things gets hard or when our path veers), our angelic entourage is always an expression of the constant Love and abiding care of God, which can reassure us on a sometimes bumpy road.

Our Guardian Angels are an expression of God and thus, infinite in expression, so we do not need to call on any other accompaniment, but we may want to.

So, who else you gonna call?

Guides

While in this book we are focused on angelic accompaniment supporting our soul mission, it should be noted that we also have guides that watch over us from the other side of the veil. We can say that they generally take two forms: friends or family members who have died and Ascended Masters—both spiritual Ascended Masters and great Masters in their fields who have ascended.

Family Members

While it can be nice to know that our Dad or Grandma or our pal Dave (hi, Dave!) is on the other side of the veil watching over us, they are perhaps not really the best resource to help us find and fulfill our soul purpose. Nothing against Uncle Al (who to me, was an Angel on Earth), but souls that have not yet "ascended" (that is, realigned completely with Source, leaving the reincarnation and karmic cycles) are not the best allies in our sacred soul work.

While each of us is (through soul) an expression of Source/God, simply dying does not make a soul completely evolved. That is why, though we may love to have our loved ones around, asking them for help along the way is not the most efficient way to go.

Of course, dying does erase The Forgetting—we all Re-member once we leave Earth—but this does not make us all-powerful and free of limitation. Only Ascended Masters access that level of freedom, of Godliness.

Why contact us at all, then? What good is there in being so connected?

So much good! Human beings who have crossed over, family and friends, who send us signs and messages (we will discuss this later) remind us that this gig here on Earth is not all there is. They remind us that we are more than meets the eye, sounding a wakeup call with regard to who we are truly (our soul, an expression of God) and to Re-membering our mission. Knowing that death does not end relationship, and that it has no power over Love, is a big step to Re-membering while we are still here on Earth, the place of The Forgetting.

But if our family and friends who have already exited the stage of life are not the best allies specifically for living our soul purpose, who you gonna call? In terms of Guides, it may be best to turn to the Ascended Masters.

Ascended Masters—Spiritual

To be clear here, the definition I am using of spiritual Ascended Master is this: Enlightened beings who have already Re-membered and fully aligned with Source. I will take a moment here to speak to something out of my particular cultural context: Christ.

49

A Word about Christ

"Holy Christmas!" I can hear my Dad now, shouting in frustration, but trying not to use the Lord's name in vain . . . and almost succeeding.

I grew up in a Catholic family, Christian, and when I was a child, the only meaning of Christ for me was Jesus. Which was already a powerful place to start, as I felt Jesus's sweet presence alongside me, His love for me (for us), as the good older brother I dreamed of as I hid in the bottom of the closet from whatever chaos was rocking our apartment at the time. So, to be clear: I am a fan.

Later, I closely studied what He actually said, always reminding us that God is our father, not just His. And always, still today, His amazing words resound in me, awe-inspiring and overwhelming: "Such works as I do you shall do also, and greater, for I have gone to the Father." (John 14:12)

How is this possible?

Jesus realized His Divinity and used it for the good, for human redemption. But as He Himself said, He made a bridge between his form and God, the realization of his soul mission. Others, too, have realized Divinity and inspired human redemption: Buddha, Mohammed, Mary, Quan Yin. These souls incarnated and then realigned for human benefit, each one rendering our path more clear, each one expressing Christ energy: Divine Love of God/Source.

The particular Ascended Masters to whom we will be attracted is not an accident! It was no accident that I was born into a Christian family but with a unique seed planted within me: the desire to explore other faiths; no accident that I had sacred experiences in church (and in my bedroom closet) that rooted me in firm "knowing" that there is more to this life than meets the eye, and that not all sacred experiences occur in a church.

Similarly, it is no accident when a different child may have had a bad experience in a similar context, thus rejecting a particular faith. All is designed to have the vessel move along a different current, one that aligns with their unique soul mission. Our vessels, beginnings, and cultural (and religious) contexts are carefully planned to optimize the possibility of realizing our soul mission.

With this understanding, the key to working with Ascended Masters (if you feel so called) is to know that if you feel an attraction to one, *follow it.* Your attraction is not an accident. There is something there for you—some treasure, some knowing, some realignment with soul and mission. Such attractions are always the seedings of the soul.

Jesus, Mary, or Joseph; Saints Francis, Clare, Therese, or Catherine; Quan Yin, Buddha, Mohammed, Lao Tsu, Padre Pio, Shiva, Shakti, Kali, Lao Tse, or Mikao Usui—culturally, we grow up with different spiritual resources, chosen by the soul and Source for us, specifically. Then, along the way, we may close to some and open to others, and these, too, are not accidental, but rather, always in accord with soul contracts. If you feel inclined to explore connection with any Ascended Master, knowing that each is a path to Source or God, allow yourself to do so.

To be clear, this does not mean that religion is not helpful; far from it. But that, too, depends on our soul path. What is clear is that religion is cultural, while spirituality is universal. The ecumenical movement in religion is a reflection of The Re-membering, the clarity that there is no place that God is not. There is only One, the Divine, Unity, Love, and Light. Thus, religion is helpful only insofar as it encourages Love, and direct connection with the Divine, with The Re-membering.

Ascended Masters—Masters in Their Field Who Have Ascended
Another often-overlooked source of support for our mission is the eternal imprint of one who has already passed on who left an imprint of mastery on Earth. Although since there is no place that God is not, all is spiritual, these beings would have mastered some human art or talent and would not necessarily be recognized as the pure expression of Source that they are.

Musicians, artists, mathematicians, even sports figures (think of a perfect gymnastic or other astounding record-making performance) can be such Masters for us. They have left this mortal coil physically but left behind the energetic imprint of their excellence: genius expressions of Source channeled, expressed, in a particular way.

We can tap into that imprint and connect and be supported by the eternal aspect of that excellence. If one is so inclined, it is precisely because there is a soul contract there. A musician might be seeking to stand on the shoulders of Ludwig van Beethoven (or John Denver), for example; a sculptor might ask Auguste Rodin for advice; a genius might stand on the shoulders of Albert Einstein—there is an astonishing breadth of Presence available to us, and if we are meant to tap into this form of assistance, it will become obvious.

What great news! We are not limited to spiritual icons or family members, when we are attracted to work with Guides that can inspire us. That said, relying on the angelic realm is more directly going to the Source of our being, and of our mission.

Archangel Mentors

In addition to our Guardian Angels and Guides, we may wish to tap into Archangelic assistance in our movement toward Re-membering.

As you know if you read my book *Inviting Angels into Your Life,* each Archangel, like our Guardian Angels, is an expression of God, or the Divine. As with all Angels, they will not intervene if we do not ask; our free will is a rule of the game, and always respected, though the request might be made to a specific Angelic Presence, or to God directly. But the beauty of working directly with the Angels and Archangels is that this allows us to more easily enter into relationship with the Divine, and thus, is effective in helping us Re-member.

Each Archangel expresses a particular frequency of the Divine, a specific Divine quality. As such, we can easily imagine that certain Archangels may bring qualities to the table that are more (or less) interesting to a particular mission.

Here, we will explore 15 Archangels with a specific view to determining which Archangels might be the right allies for our personal soul mission. Ready?

Archangel Michael: Protectors and Lightworkers

Archangel Michael, often pictured with a sword, expresses the Power (of Love) of God. His goal is Transformation—transforming the fear that plagues the earth and creating space for Love. Stalwart, powerful, protective, Michael assists souls that call on Him in all work that protects and defends others, such as police, soldiers, firefighters, emergency workers, bodyguards, crossing guards, etcetera.

The mentorship of Michael is not just limited to those in these obvious roles of protection in society; Michael is also known to be the mentor (or boss) of all Lightworkers! Recognizing that a soul that expresses as a Lightworker is here to bring Light into darkness and Love to transform fear, we see a natural alliance between a Lightworker's purpose and that of Michael. As such, Archangel Michael is perhaps the Archangelic ally or mentor for someone who recognizes themselves as a Lightworker (you, perhaps?).

Confused about where to go, what to do? In addition to getting clarity by doing the exercises in this book, asking Michael for assistance can help us to understand and achieve next steps on our journey in alignment with our specific soul plan and mission.

Archangel Raphael: Healers

Another well-known Archangelic mentor is Archangel Raphael, who expresses the Healing of God. As such He is a great mentor and ally for all in the health and healing field, both traditional and holistic: doctors, nurses, therapists, hospital workers and technicians, palliative caretakers, researchers, and all healing practitioners in all expression.

It should be noted, however, that the Healing of God, Divine healing, is not exactly that to which we humans often refer as healing; that is, an eradication of the symptoms of sickness. Instead, Divine healing is more an alignment with the Divine, which is not the same!

In the first case, we can experience symptoms that are relieved, and be happy about that, unless or until those symptoms return. Modern medicine is great at relieving symptoms, but sometimes it does so without treating the root of the problem, or by adding other symptoms.

Whether physical, mental, emotional, or spiritual, all sickness is the result of an energetic imbalance. Adding something to the system via drugs, for example, does not transform the underlying imbalance but, rather, adds something that temporarily hides the imbalance. While it can temporarily bring about a sort of balance and relieve symptoms, this temporary or artificial solution is not true healing; if we need to keep taking a drug for the rest of our lives, underlying healing has not happened. To be clear, this is not to tear down such treatments. Sometimes they are indeed needed. But this is not what Raphael, Divine healing, is about.

Divine healing seeks to balance the underlying problem, or to align us with the truth that there is already balance there. Huh?

Knowing that there is no coincidence, ever, on a soul's journey to Re-membering, no sickness is an accident. Each is a gift, even when (man, oh man!) sometimes it is hard to see it that way.

Either a sickness is a gift that is inviting (or forcing!) us to balance what needs balancing (diet, work/play, stress, etcetera), or it is a gift that the soul chose because the sickness itself is in alignment with the chosen soul mission.

In the first case, examples abound of burnout and depression, heart conditions, backaches—conditions that force a vessel (human form) to undergo a sea change, to slow down or completely change directions. This is always in line with the soul's mission, even when it is not in line with the human being's ambitions.

In the second case, we find people who experience difficult life situations; children and adults dealing with grave and chronic illness in alignment with their soul mission. As discussed earlier, such people impact those around them, inviting the cultivation of compassion, and/or allowing souls to perhaps balance karma; or maybe their resources will be used to find a cure for them, and thus for others. So many possibilities! We do not always understand the why of it, but there are Archangel mentors (like Metatron, who we will see in a bit) who can help us with understanding.

Archangel Gabriel: Communicators and Clairvoyants, Mothers

Archangel Gabriel expresses perfectly Divine Communication. As such, She—of course, Angels do not have gender, but Gabriel (or Gabrielle) is a feminine, receptive energy—is a great mentor or ally for those in fields of communication: writers, speakers, journalists, entertainers, mentalists, mediums, etcetera.

Additionally, Gabrielle carries the soft communication of Love that is Divine Mother energy. As such, She is a wonderful ally for working with children or inner child work (as we will see in Chapter 7).

Gabrielle helps with both Divine and human communication. She can help us by bringing our human communications into alignment with the highest frequency available to us at any given time, and thus, is great to ask for assistance if we have difficult news to deliver, or if we are in a communication function in the world.

That said, She also helps with Divine communication, including the (re)opening of our clairvoyant gifts or clairaudience, clairvoyance, clairsentience, and claircognizance (intuition), allowing us to see, feel, hear, and know beyond what might be considered "normal." We will discuss these later in more detail, but for now, suffice it to say that these gifts are not just normal but integral to, and part and parcel of, our Re-membering.

Archangel Jophiel: Artists and Creators

Archngel Jophiel is the Beauty of God, and as such, even though She is not a household name, we can imagine that everyone has experienced Her Presence at some moment or another. As one would imagine, Jophiel is an excellent partner for artists: those whose life purpose/soul mission is expressed through creating art and beauty on Earth. But Jophiel's Presence is not just for those who consider themselves artists; rather, She is here for all of us, at some level, helping us to Re-member to see the beauty in our creation. She reminds us that it is we who are responsible for our lives; we create them!

Each of us is a child of the Creator; as such, we create. We can't help it; it's in our DNA. What is news to some people, however, and part of *all* our Re-membering, is that we create all the time, consciously as well as unconsciously. We create with our actions, certainly, but also with our thoughts, emotions, and words. What we express in these ways emanates from us and fills our energetic field. What is in our energetic field creates in accordance with the Law of Energy that "Energy seeks equilibrium."

We attract that which resonates with the energy around us; what does not resonate is blocked. Each word that leaves our lips carries the energy of creation. Each thought emanates its high or low energy. Each emotion, from high to low frequency and everything in between, is rooted in a thought that engendered it and fills our energy field. In these ways, through the quality of our thoughts, words, and emotions, we either support or block our soul mission and our human dreams.

Once we Re-member this, we can truly bring about change; with the help of Jophiel, we can clean up our emanation and create consciously with our words, artists of our own masterpiece: our life!

Archangel Zadkiel: Mediators and Peacemakers

Archange Zadkiel is known as the Archangel who expresses the Forgiveness of God, helping us to see, feel, hear, or know every situation from God's eternal perspective, allowing Re-membering. Zadkiel helps us to look at things from that higher perspective, and to release anything that is not in alignment with the highest.

On Earth, He is an excellent mentor for peacemakers and mediators, intermediaries in social and societal systems. But not only this! He is also a wonderful mentor for those who carry the burden of non-forgiveness, in situations where we carry burdens of the past into the present.

When we are burdened by the wrongs (theirs or ours) of the past, we are not available in the present to live our Highest life, our highest expression, our mission! In line with another Law of Energy, "Where our attention goes, so goes our energy that creates," when we are still angry or hurt or hurting over events from the past, we are stuck there! It is impossible to Re-member, to align with our soul and mission, when we are stuck in low energies of the past.

Working with Zadkiel brings us gently back into the truth of innocence (ours and others') from the eternal perspective, Re-membering that we are eternal souls in temporary role play here on Earth. Even the very worst experiences that mark us are soul contracts, and Zadkiel can help us to release them.

With a little help from our Friends in High Places, we will even be able to see how even these bad experiences have served us.

Archangel Metatron: Teachers and Learners

Metatron is the Archangelic Presence that expresses Divine wisdom and understanding. As such, He is a natural mentor for those who are attracted to learning and to teaching. Both those in a teaching profession and students on any level can benefit from the help of Metatron.

In addition, even if we are not currently teachers or students, we are always learning and teaching; it goes with the terrain here on Earth. If there is something our soul needs us to learn (for karmic reasons, for example, or directly in line with our broader mission), we will have the experience over and over until we learn what we need in order to be able to move on. This is the answer to the perennial question, "Why does this keep happening to me?" Ask Metatron for understanding.

Whether a situation is recurring or deeply disturbing, we can ask Metatron to help us gain insight into it, simply by asking, and then listen deeply and openly to hear the answer. Such experiences always help us to Re-member.

Archangel Sandalphon: Musicians and Singers

Archangel Sandalphon is the Music or Song of God and, as such, is an excellent ally for all musicians and singers, professional or otherwise.

But He also helps any of us who call on him to recognize our body as our instrument, and to learn how to play it. This is the seat of Re-membering: dis-identifying with the body and instead, learning to see it (and love it and play it) as our sacred instrument.

Sometimes, the world teaches us that there is no place for our voice, either our singing voice or our truth. This is again part of the imposed Forgetting. In duality, even as there are forces of Light like the Angels inviting us to Re-member, there are other forces trying to keep us in the dark. But our voice is always crucial to our mission, whether we are here to sing or share our unique perspective.

Song is the high frequency of Joy, and so finding our authentic voice is important for the expression of our soul's Joy, Light, and Love on the earth at this time. Remembering that all voices are of God (whether the world recognizes that or not) is key to creating new harmonies in the fabric of time, with each instrument playing its unique piece!

Archangel Ariel: Landscapers and Gardeners

Archangel Ariel is the Archangel most closely associated with Nature and the elemental energies sometimes called fairies. She is a powerhouse, and only available to humans who have Re-membered that we are co-guardians of the earth, here to protect and love our environment. As such, she is an excellent mentor for those who work in ecology, or with water or land in any way, as long as it is with an attitude of Love and respect.

Ariel is also here for us if our soul is calling us to be in coherence with that role of protection of the earth, as we stretch toward a world of less waste and consumption and more appreciation of the earth and her beauties.

This includes sensitive souls who may feel a strong connection to elemental energies, as many are here in this lifetime who perhaps feel more connected to flowers, animals, and trees than they do to other human beings. If this is the case, often it is because in a recent lifetime, these souls were expressing as elementals/fairies, but who, seeing that the earth needed protection from human blindness, decided on the soul level to take on human form to come to her rescue.

All who work with Ariel bring humanity back into balance with their relationship with the earth, and so many Lightworkers are called in this direction these days. Thank you!

Archangel Uriel: Emergency Workers and Emergers

Archangel Uriel, the Fire of God, is no joking matter! He is present whenever there is fire or any type of storm or catastrophe, natural or otherwise. In this period of wildfires, floods, pandemics, earthquakes, economic meltdowns, and personal upheavals, this Presence of God is active on Earth. As such, He is a great ally for those who work in the world as first responders, emergency medical technicians, firefighters, or anyone who provides assistance in times of trouble.

In addition, He is there for those of us feeling the tumult of such times, reminding us to Re-member: to know that "accidents" are not accidental; that everything that happens helps us in the Flow toward our soul mission, even when we are not aware of it.

As a field that has been burned is rendered more fertile, so, too, once the "fires" of our lives are out and things are calm, such situations give us new eyes to see and the inspiration to rebuild, to Re-member, to rise from the ashes. We can ask Uriel to help us with the high dramas of life, give us a heads-up when possible, grant us cool heads in the midst of the fire and fury, and afterward help with the Re-membering and reconstructing, ever more in alignment with our truth.

Archangel Azrael: Undertakers and Mediums

Let's be clear: Archangel Azrael, also known as the Angel of Death, does not kill us.

Now that we've got that out of the way, what Azrael does do is shine His great bright light to guide us from here to "there" at the moment of our death, making clear the path homeward. Azrael guards the (rapidly thinning) veil that separates our daily life on Earth and the eternal truth of life. As such, He is an excellent ally for any humans who accompany the dying (or their loved ones) through the sometimes unclear and difficult process of releasing our attachment to this life so we can get back to our eternal home. Doctors, nurses, therapists, palliative caretakers, undertakers, and anyone who lightens the burden of the dying or their families through the process would do well to have their path supported and their burden eased by Azrael.

But since we all will meet Azrael when the time comes, perhaps we all would do well to call on Azrael, for if we recognize Him when the time does come, it will make our own passing that much more peaceful.

Additionally, there are many "death" periods during this life, times when we could use the help and support of one that helps us to Re-member that the truth of who we are is not in this time and space form, but a soul that is eternal, an expression of Source, Love, and Light. Such situations include but are not limited to great times of change and rebirth, such as the loss of a loved one or a job or moving home or country or relationship.

Archangel Chamuel: Researchers and Seekers

Archangel Chamuel (sometimes called Samuel), He who seeks God, supports all human seeking, which is the precursor to all human Re-membering. As such, He is an excellent mentor for professional seekers, such as researchers and detectives.

He is an excellent ally for anyone, since we all seek something, from time to time. Whether it be the keys to the car or to the kingdom, a parking spot or a spot to park and lay down some roots, peace on Earth or a moment's peace in a busy day—Chamuel can help us. Why not ask?

There are those who say that Angels have better things to do than to help us with finding "stuff." Oh, really?

Imagine if a part of God was unconscious and, like a bull in a china shop, created havoc all over the place. Now, imagine if that part of God is us (because it is). Exactly! Angels have every interest in helping us to calm down, slow down, and Re-member.

Think of how you felt the last time you lost your keys or your wallet, or couldn't find a parking spot. Now, remember that we create with our words, emotions, and thoughts. What did *you* create, in those moments? Light and peace?

Exactly! Thank you, Chamuel.

Archangel Jeremiel: Life Coaches and Dreamers

Archangel Jeremiel is the presence of God that greets us when Azrael brings us from here to "there." He guides our life review, during which we are not judged (the judging and the punishment happens here on earth, in the duality that makes such things seem possible); rather, we are guided by this celestial life coach into seeing clearly what worked on our paths in relation to the original soul plan and mission, and what didn't. If the plan succeeded, and the mission was completed, at this point the next evolutionary mission (if there will be one), begins to come into being. However, if the mission did not succeed, a new life plan with the same or somewhat modified mission will be put in place, taking into consideration all experience gained and any karma incurred.

We can see how Jeremiel could be a great ally for a life coach looking to guide and assist a client in finding what works and doesn't work on their path. In fact, any of us can ask Jeremiel to help us out with a life review midstream during this lifetime.

Another specificity of Jeremiel is that He helps people who are dreamers understand their clairvoyant dreams. In simpler cultures, shamans or leaders once used (some still do) what is called "the dreaming" to gain access to higher wisdom for their tribe or community. The Dreaming is making a wider-world comeback, so if you feel you have this gift, Jeremiel is a great ally to have.

But how do we know when a dream is a message? (Most dreams are not; most are simply the mind taking out the garbage at the end of the day.)

A dream that is a message will have one or more of these characteristics:

- *It stays with us.* The emotions or images remain with us the whole day or beyond.
- *It is recurring.* The soul sends lessons again and again until we get what we need.
- *There is great emotion.* We may wake up crying or laughing or both.
- *A visit from a deceased loved one or an Ascended Master* may occur.

If you are a dreamer, it is a good time to team up with Jeremiel; perhaps your dreaming can serve your mission, and also humanity.

Archangel Haniel: Healers and Sensitives

Archangel Haniel, the Grace of God, carries natural healing energy by grace to all who request it. If you are in the world to do such natural healing, attracted to working with essential oils, homeopathy, crystals, or sound and light (to name a few), Haniel is a wonderful ally and mentor. If you have read my book *Discover Your Crystal Family: Working with Stones and Their Angelic Messengers,* you already know what a great ally Haniel can be.

But for all sensitives, She is a good friend to have, as She reminds us to play our instruments wisely, gently, and with grace. Haniel is linked to the moon. Her silvery light reminds those who see such things of a bright harvest moon, shining full in the night. Haniel reminds us to remember that like the moon, we have phases. Contrary to what the world urges us to do, we move in a natural ebb and flow and cannot continue going at 100 percent all the time, 24/7. Only by allowing our fallow time can we stand in our power and align with our shining, our soul mission. If or when we forget to allow that fallow time, luckily there is an Archangel that can help.

Archangel Raguel: Justice and Balance

Archangel Raguel, Justice of God, brings us aid in any legal situations on Earth if we ask. As such, He is a great mentor for those who work in law and justice: police, lawyers, judges, jailers, mediators, and for anyone who finds themselves stuck in the mire of legal process.

He is also a mentor for anyone who works in social justice, aiding those to whom life has dealt a bleak hand, balancing the scales somewhat, if you will.

Finally, He helps brings balance to our physical being. He is a great resource when the imbalance of the world has us tired out and lacking enthusiasm. If we ask Raguel for an energetic boost, He will always respond, filling us directly, so we can be filled with God, enthusiastic and energetic once again. All we need to do is ask and then wait, deeply open for the filling. (I highly recommend this practice!)

Archangel Raziel: Leaders and Gurus

Archangel Raziel, Secret of God, works more closely with our soul than with us in our human form, and so often comes into play in our lifetimes when we have already begun The Re-membering. As such, He is an excellent ally for spiritual teachers and seekers, leaders, and gurus; also for leaders in any function who want to lead in alignment with the highest values.

He reminds us of the difference between a Leader and a leader, a Guru and a guru: a leader wants others to follow them, while a Leader inspires others to lead. A guru wants others to know how powerful he or she (the guru) is, while a Guru wants others to know and experience their *own* power, in unity.

Onward

And now, accompanied by Angels and Guides, family members and friends, Ascended Masters and Masters who have ascended, the question arises: What about our soul? Can't we ask our soul for help?

Of course we can! A Stradivarius, amazing violin that it is, cannot play itself. We as instruments can play ourselves, but for the music to be beautiful, let's ask the soul for help.

Chapter 4
SOUL MISSION—
OUR LIFE PURPOSE

So far, we have looked at how souls envisage their life's mission on Earth in co-creation with God/Source and then embark on their intrepid journey as human beings. We have looked at how our personal context from birth was meticulously planned, and how our form and our strengths and weaknesses all support the realization of the mission that our soul has chosen.

We have even explored the Divine assistance that is always ready to help us, especially our Guardian Presence and Archangels, if we would but call upon them. But what about calling on our souls, ourselves?

When we pierce the illusion of separation, we may get a glimpse of the unity that underlies the truth: There is no place that God is not. But when it is time (and it is, perhaps, if you are reading this), can we recognize that the soul who chose us *is* us, the truth of who we are? Can we (and do we even want to) realign with that Divine aspect of ourselves to more easily fulfill the purpose for which we were born? Well, all that might take a bit of time to get used to, *non?*

Exactly!

The first step in coming into alignment with our Divine aspect and thus, our purpose, is to recognize that we are perfectly on time. We are not meant to undo years of forgetfulness in one fell swoop; rather, we are meant to allow the haze of The Forgetting to lift slowly, steadily, at a rhythm that allows us to grow accustomed to who we are in a delightful fashion. No rush, no fear. Recognizing that we were gradually embedded into the world's limited vision of our life here on Earth, the most peaceful (and so the highest and best) way of undoing The Forgetting is to do so over time. So, no matter how eager we might be for change and fulfillment, in this book we will do what the Angels suggest we do, in general; that is, take things slowly and easily. One step at a time, we will move steadily forward, peacefully.

Soul Mission versus Life Purpose

In Chapter 2, we discussed at length what sorts of missions souls might embark on, and the myriad ways these missions may be lived out—or not, as the ground rule here on Earth is that all humans have free will.

Further, we looked at those of us who are Lightworkers and our mission: to bring Light into darkness, hope into despair, Love into fear (basically, the Prayer of St. Francis). While we have a sense of what the soul is looking for here, since we know that free will (literally) rules, what about human beings? Do we get to have a say about all this?

So glad you asked!

Outside of when we are born, our circumstances, and when and how we die, we have a say in everything! Nothing happens unless we allow it on some level. Whether or not a human being is aware of our soul (most really aren't, not really), we choose. Even choosing to do nothing or believe we have no choice is, well, a choice. When we are solidly in the haze of The Forgetting, chances are pretty good that we will never align with our soul mission, so great can be the worry and fear surrounding us. This is often why so many people die with regret; they were too afraid to live.

This is also why depression is the fastest growing sickness in the Western world, and why burnouts are multiplying. When our choices distance us from our soul mission, something inside us suffers. There is no logic to it, so society has no good response. (Drugging us is not, I would argue, a "good" response, although I recognize that, in the short term, this can be a way to get over the hump as we realign and readjust.)

The rise in cases of depression and burnout is not because we are weaker than previous generations, but rather, because we are in an evolutionary time for humanity and our stronger sensitivity is pushing us to other ways of being. Continuing a way of living that was molded in the past is less and less tenable, and if we force ourselves to be what the world wants us to be, it can be disastrous for our health and well-being.

Knowing that we always have the final word with regard to our path, then, it is perhaps a good idea to differentiate between *soul mission* and *life purpose,* as we use them here:

Our *soul mission* is the objective the soul has chosen this lifetime through you, in co-creation with God; the human role in carrying out our soul mission is our *life purpose*—how we as human beings on the planet will align with that mission, or not!

For example, a sensitive soul might be here to play a Lightworker role, but perhaps that very sensitivity is creating fear, causing them to "hide out" from that mission (I know whereof I speak; we can hide out in so many ways). Activities that diminish our sensitivity constitute "hiding out": drugs, alcohol, gambling, too much exercise, too much work, too much social media, too much TV; in fact, anything that desensitizes us. You get the picture.

In line with the Universal Law of Energy that states, "Where our attention goes, so goes our energy," when we throw ourselves into any habit to an extreme, there is no space left for welcoming in the new. Thus, by hiding out in this way, we may remain stuck in The Forgetting, either consciously or unconsciously.

While some of us fall into such traps unconsciously, I can personally attest that some of us are conscious that we are putting off what is important and not taking the path that awaits us. This is sometimes done out of fear—fear of change is the poison gas that keeps many in The Forgetting or the avoidance of Re-membering; however, such avoidance can also be rooted in anger, especially if the world has been harsh toward us in the past. Imagining that the big bad world does not deserve our Light can make us even more stuck in The Forgetting, and this can go on for a long, long time.

Many of the souls arriving on the planet now have more resilience and are born with the desire to change the world, and so they shall. But those of us who are already here are preparing the way, and any one of us who awakens to the mission and aligns with it, making of it our human purpose, contributes greatly to the shifting to come.

A human being can, of course, align "accidentally" with the soul mission (or not so accidentally), as we have seen earlier. For example, if a soul is here to express music, it will have chosen a vessel gifted in that, perhaps born to a musical family, setting the scene for the human to choose a life of music, seemingly of their own free will. A prodigy is not necessarily wondering if their soul chose the path or if *they* did; they are already en route, and thus, life purpose aligns to soul mission.

But if we are not a born prodigy, how can we connect with our soul mission? Further, are we sure that is a good idea? What do we humans get out of the deal?

All good questions! When I was starting out, a rather stubborn streak in me regularly posed such questions, keeping soul level honest. It is incumbent upon us to take our free will seriously, to enjoy it to the full, but standing in our free will and human power does not mean that we should reject out of hand the journey being proposed by our soul. Far from it!

Tracing the journey of the soul's choosing is a fulfilling and Joyful way to live. A human does not submit to the will of the soul, but rather, embraces it with Joy, because it is delightful and meaningful and in perfect harmony with our instrument; the human being role we are here to play.

We discussed earlier that when a new person, place, or situation is (oddly) familiar, it is an indicator that we are treading a path foreseen by our soul. But that is not the only time we can be sure of our progress toward fulfilling the life purpose and soul mission that is ours. We can also be confident of it when we experience the "sweet spot" and "the flow."

The Sweet Spot

Think about a time when you found "the sweet spot"—you know, when everything was flowing and going your way. In sport, maybe you couldn't miss a shot, or you felt like you could run forever, pure power and speed. In song, maybe your voice opened and soared, a delight and surprise to your own ears and heart. In music, maybe you felt like you and the instrument were playing as one. At work . . .

Wait a minute! Back up there! What was that, just before "at work"?

"In music, you felt like you and the instrument were one . . ."

Yes, that's it! When we are talking about soul mission and life purpose, the sweet spot is exactly that: when you (the soul) and the instrument (you, the human being) are one; those moments when your choosing and the soul's plan coincide and are sweet, no matter how long they last, just for some moments, or maybe for a good while. No matter! If you have ever had this feeling, you know! The sweet spot is somehow imprinted in us, always recognizable.

Like the "sweet spot" on a baseball bat, golf club, or tennis racket, when we hit our sweet spot everything happens easily, perfectly, Joyfully.

Our human sweet spot experiences are specifically designed to lead us in the direction of our soul mission. Sweet spots aren't called "sweet" for nothing. It feels good to be in the sweet spot, and we humans are often motivated by feeling good. Even though the world sometimes tries to get us to do things by obligation (you *should* go to this school, you *shouldn't* be an artist, you *should* get a steady job, you *shouldn't* marry for love, you *should* think about money), when we listen to the world instead of our heart, we step away from our sweet spot, our Joy. Such choices can result in depression, which really is a measure of how far from our sweet spot, our soul highest path, we have strayed.

Sweet spots are moments of Re-membering, where the soul and its human aspect align.

Going back to the beginning of this book, sweet spot experiences include moments when we meet someone for the first time but it doesn't feel like the first time. When we meet someone, and maybe even feel magnetically drawn to them, for example. The fabled soul mates!

A Word about Soul Mates

It is important to note that being magnetically drawn to someone does not necessarily mean the two people are meant to be together, as a couple, or for life. It does, however, mean that they are meant to be on each other's paths, that there is a soul contract in the offing. We have something to learn from the interaction, and the magnetism ensures that we pursue it. Unfortunately, until recently, we humans were only conditioned to recognize energetic attraction as romantic ties, and so often, such attraction is misconstrued as being a soul mate relationship. (The truth is, there is not just one soul mate on a planet of 8 billion souls, as much as the idea is charming.) What can be said about romantic relationships is that they, too, are soul contracts. We don't end up with someone for no reason. Allowing the soul contract to be what it is, instead of forcing it into worldly expectations of coupledom, is the best way of allowing the soul contract to express as it is meant to, allowing peace and Joy.

As we have seen, our life path as a human being *always* coincides with the will of the soul with God, at least at two points: the very beginning of life (with the choice of our form and birth setting) and at the end (we never die but that the soul is in accord with the ending of the life journey), as well as any sweet spots we might encounter, including but not limited to moments of illogical familiarity with people, places, or things (when we meet people and feel we know them, or if we go to a place for the first time and somehow feel at home there).

But there is yet another way of recognizing where our soul is inviting us along the way, best called "The Flow."

The Flow   When a Decision Isn't a Decision

Think of a life marker on your path, something that in your past changed everything   maybe a choice of college, a job, or a geographic move, such as changing cities or countries. It may have been the choice of partner or best friend or course of study.

The key is to think of a time in the past when you made a decision, a choice, that wasn't really a choice, but so obvious to you that it was a foregone conclusion—a decision that wasn't really a decision!

There are a couple of examples in my own life that come to mind. I went to Georgetown's School of Foreign Service pre-internet and sight unseen, rejecting all other university suitors. There, I studied Humanities in International Relations, even though everybody said that was a lame choice if I wanted to be employable afterward. When the bank offered me a job in London, I said immediately that I would go only if it were Paris (where all my clients were), and when they said yes, I left my home and country without a second thought.

While that last bit might paint me to be not very sentimental, the opposite is true. I am still in strong friendships with the people I left behind when I came to Europe. It was just not even a question, at the time; as if I had been waiting my whole life for just that. These choices were obvious, no hesitation. Have you had any like that?

In relationships, too, at times we benefit from the obvious: meeting someone who we know will be a good friend or who we know we will marry, or a teacher with whom we know we are meant to study.

When a decision is more like a natural occurrence than an active choice, we can be sure that it is happening in alignment with our soul mission. Flow brings with it synchronicities, or fortuitous events that open doors, and even though we might be tempted to call them coincidences, they are not.

In The Flow, things happen naturally, effortlessly, we feel blessed, and thus, become a blessing to those around us. That is not to say that everything is easy when we are aligned with soul. We are still in duality on Earth (which means that things can be both hard and easy), so that may not be the case. Do the easy experiences come more often as we go with The Flow? Do things that would have seemed terribly hard in the past become easier? Well, not so much! If things happen more easily, it doesn't mean that we do nothing, and of course, just because something seems clear, this doesn't mean we don't have a choice.

Of course, we always have a choice. Free will reigns! But these Flow events are so fluid and simple and inviting that we most often choose them—unless the world gets in our head, and in our way.

For example, when I told my parents about the Paris job offer, my father tried to dissuade me. Even as my mother said, "Of course, you should go. This has been your dream," my father stood behind her and vigorously shook his head. History had already taught me that my dad never wanted me to take a step away, so I laughed gently . . . and listened to my mother!

When we find The Flow in our lives, it is important to flow with it and let it carry our vessel (us) to our next phase of life and purpose. If we remain alert in The Flow, we are carried to opportunities both for our fulfillment and the fulfillment of our soul mission. But in the duality that is Earth, every time we stretch to our Light, darkness will react to dissuade and distract us. Sometimes that darkness is called Dad; other times, teachers; other times, spouse or friends. Going against such currents bring us to the toughest aspect of going with our Flow: *People won't like it!*

If we find our flow and go with it, you can be sure that at least some people won't like it. Like my dad in the above anecdote, people are not really happy for us when we go with The Flow, especially if that Flow makes us grow, or makes us go away.

You see, folks like things to be stable. Imagine that we are paddling a separate canoe with every single person in our life. Since energy always seeks equilibrium, we have found some stability with each person in the relationship canoe, but then we rock the boat!

When we go with The Flow and grow, life becomes easier; we become more confident and, thus, powerful with each passing stage. Hopefully, there will be people in our lives who cheer us on, but there will very likely also be some that don't, because our movement rocks their boat, too!

When we break out of the mold and the stability of who we were and what we were doing (and where), it will rock each of the canoes we are in, the relationships we have. Very often, people won't like it! They might miss us if we physically leave, or they might be unhappy that we have stepped into our Light, shining the spotlight also on them.

When we align with soul and step out of the blanket fort in which we may have been hiding, it has a big impact energetically on those with whom we are in relationship. Unintentionally, unconsciously, our movement rocks their stability, and energetically (since energy seeks equilibrium), it is as though we are poking them, prodding them into waking.

Since energy seeks equilibrium, our aligning to our own Light evokes their Light as well (everybody's got some!), whether they are ready to stand in it or not. If fear outweighs their desire for that Light, they will resist flowing with you to their own Light and might try to obstruct your path as well.

This explains why so many of us who open to alignment with our soul mission find that folks, well, leave.

Those that leave may not say a word but simply distance themselves. If asked, often they won't be able to put their finger on it, but the truth is, they just can't stand being around us. It would be easy to attribute this to jealousy, but it is more than that (and as we will see later, jealousy is maybe not what we think it is at all).

The truth is, when we choose consciously to align with our soul and The Flow, we can make people uncomfortable without intending it. Our Light is like an alarm going off (one with a spotlight!). As we know, not everybody loves to wake up when the alarm goes off. Whereas once our relationship canoes with friends, colleagues, family, or mates were stable, now they may have become too unstable for the canoe ride together. Has your aligning with your soul mission already cost some relationships?

The good news is that we never lose anyone, as all are One. After this dance on Earth is over, we will all have a good chuckle over it. The even better news is that when some people leave, new people arrive—people who are more in sync with our new energetic. And sometimes, people leave and then come around again. None of what they do is our business. Let each soul find their way, beautifully.

Of course, this does not mean that we need to abandon longstanding friendships or family relationships. It does mean that if we are growing, we need to be really aware of the shifting dynamics of our canoes, knowing that some may need gentle attention to keep afloat, and others may need to be carried ashore to rest awhile away from the water because of the fast Flow of the river.

People we love stay people we love if we don't (in our fear) hang on too tight when natural movements create space between us. If we fight this, trying to swim upstream, it can create rancor in one or the other or both, sullying the Love that had once been and crashing the canoe!

In my work, I find that couples who split up gently when their values and objectives are no longer in sync tend to remain close friends, Love intact, though not romantic coupledom. However, if one or the other (or both), is too afraid of a separation, they strangle the Love and kill it. Even if they stay together, the juice, the Joy of the soul contract, is gone.

Getting Back the Mojo

So, when we have lost connection with our soul and mission, when our purpose is fuzzy and the haze of Forgetting is like a thick pea soup, how can we get our mojo back? How can we find the sweet spot and renew our Flow, so that synchronicities daily assure us that we are on the right path?

Paying attention and watching for sweet spots and welcoming them, saying yes to doors flying open for us, and letting go of what was as we move forward will always shift things back into movement.

How do we find a sweet spot? Listen to small notions that don't make sense, such as, *I'd like to walk down this street to see what is there,* or *I could really use a nap,* or *It's been a while since I called Wies.* Noticing inclinations that seem to come out of nowhere can adjust our perspective, so that the prow of our "canoe" catches a current, bringing us back into The Flow.

But what about when inspiration runs dry? What if we feel like we have really lost the juice? I often have clients who come see me for this very reason. It can hurt to feel like you have lost the juicy sweet spot, once you have found it, and once spiritual connection with soul is in place, we miss it terribly if we stray off the path into a dry spell.

Dry Spells

Many of my clients speak to a common phenomenon that I like to call "dry spells." They feel sad or angry or confused, because they had experienced the sweet spot of soul connection, and connection with their Angels in the past, but it seems to have dried up!

Some look to cast blame—on God, the Angels, loved ones, black magic curses, or even themselves. They feel that sacred connection has dried up and look for reasons, blame maybe, but above all, solutions, ways to get it back. Of course, such limiting beliefs fill their energetic field, which attracts only more of the same, keeping the person from a lifting of the veil, which is hidden in the dry spell experience.

I am always happy to work with such folks, as a simple shift in perspective can often do the trick!

In Nature, a dry spell is a time when a lack of rain dries out the land, rendering it less fertile for creation. The saving grace of rain is the only real remedy for Nature's dry spells. But for humans on a spiritual path, the news is better! Since all progress to Re-membering is a grace, a dose of understanding of what is really going on can shift our energy and thus, our sacred experience.

There are two things to remember here, both very helpful:

- *God's Plan.* Everything truly happens for a good evolutionary reason, even when we can't see it.
- *Part of the Process.* The "dry spell" is actually a deepening; step two of a three-step process to deepened spiritual experience, ecstatic awakening, slowing/dry spell, and deepened Re-membering.

God's Plan

We have perhaps all heard the old saying that "Everything happens for a reason." Maybe you, like me, have even been frustrated by glib assurances on the part of those around us (I am hearing my mother say it right now, though she is long deceased!) that all is in God's plan. But the truth is, as frustrating as it feels when we are not happy with the way things are unfolding, it is true! And God's plan for us is always the soul's plan for us, and always the path that will bring us as humans the most Joy, our "sweet spot!"

Nothing is an accident. Everything that happens on Earth is an opportunity to advance on our path of Re-membering, of alignment with our mission, even when we can't see it because we thought we knew better. Thinking that we know what is best for us (and maybe for everybody else, too!) is a hazard of the human "job," but who is better placed to see all ramifications of everything, us or God?

I always chuckle at myself, thanks to the following pearl of wisdom given me by my mentor, Sister Regina Bechtle, a Sister of Charity and spiritual guide, poet and author: Whenever I feel like something that *is* shouldn't be (that is, whenever I think God is wrong and I am right . . . LOL), I look up to the heavens, addressing God out loud, saying: "Are You sure about this? Because I think I have a better idea!" Without fail, I chuckle. Something deep inside recognizes how silly it is to question what is, to flail against what is happening, to go against The Flow of the soul plan, God's plan.

To be clear, this does not mean that we don't oppose injustice if we meet it on the road! But even in opposing injustice, we can perhaps welcome edification (maybe with the help of Metatron?) to see and feel and know why a given situation is arising.

Let's look at an example: discrimination in the world. The idea is not that we accept discrimination but that we see situations where discrimination expresses, even violently, as useful in terms of human evolution, from a higher perspective. If such ugliness remained hidden, how could it be healed? When it is expressed, our deep revulsion leads humanity (slowly, perhaps, but surely) out of it, into true healing.

The disgusting metaphor of a pimple comes to mind. A pimple must come to the surface and explode before it is wholly healed. If it only recedes and hides anew, it cannot yet be healed. So even though no one with a heart can be happy at discriminatory division and violence, we can access a higher perspective and see how it can serve—is serving—evolution. Thus, it may well inspire us to actively oppose injustice, steeling us against the lassitude of fatalism and despair, knowing that the worse it is, the closer we are to the true healing and unity that is always God's plan!

On a personal level, who hasn't had the experience of being sad that someone (perhaps a lover, friend, or family member) or something (a job, maybe) exited our life, only to realize later that it was for the best? I know I have! Even if we were "sure" that it was a bad thing, such departures create space for something better, more in line with our mission and the sweet spot of Joy to arise!

Death

When a loved one dies, of course, this is always hard to swallow, but knowing that the veil is just that, through such a "loss," we can access a gain. A deeper, more eternal connection with a loved one that is still "here" for us can occur if we can only relax into such a passing; however, if we get caught up in the drama (as most of us do, the Western world culture not emphasizing a continuity), we may not be able to access the deeper connection that can now be revealed.

A silly but effective metaphor comes to mind. Imagine we have a pet snake (I wouldn't, but here we go anyway). Imagine our pet snake molts; that is, sheds its skin. Imagine then that we are inconsolable, rending our clothing, tearing our hair, gnashing our teeth, sitting vigil with the skin that has been cast off, so much so that we don't notice the newly revitalized snaky-poo that is slithering around us!

The death of a loved one is akin to this. It can lead us into high drama, then emptiness, and then, perhaps, if we are willing to let go of the first two stages, a deepening of connection that reminds us that we never lose anyone, that we are all always connected.

A Dry Spell after Loss

After the initial shock and sorrow pass, the death of a loved one can also lead us into a feeling akin to a spiritual "dry spell," as life can feel empty. This sense of emptiness can, in fact, engender a spiritual dry spell and its accompanying despair, but even that will serve, if we allow it to, as God's plan is always perfect. Let's look at those three steps now.

1 Ecstatic Awakening

When we first awaken to our spiritual paths, it is all very exciting. The feeling of *ennui* with this world falls away, and our Joy is stimulated. We become like sponges thirsty for sacred experience—perhaps reading everything we can get our hands on or learning from those farther along the path than us (thank you Barbara Uboe, my first; you always remember your first!) or signing up for workshops and group learning. Group work really helps, letting us know that all this excitement and these new sensations are normal. We can feel "high" with connection, confirmation that life is indeed magic. Sacred experience comes easily, and our clairvoyant gifts open, facilitating communication across the veil. Very exciting!

2 Slowing /Dry Spell

Some time afterward, depending on the person, things slow down. The daily spiritual practice (if there is one) will likely become quieter, with fewer tears, fewer visions, less ecstasy, etcetera. Our experiences will seem calmer and may feel less exciting. If we have grown dependent on the excitement, this can be disappointing, and in that disappointment, communication that was fluid may seem to dry up. At this time, frustration may mount. A person who does not know that this is normal may feel lost or abandoned and even fall into depression (which renders sacred communication completely inaccessible for the duration) and remain stuck in it for a while.

There are two important things to understand about this common experience: First, it is normal that our instrument/bodies are less dramatically impacted by high frequency sacred experience as we go along, because our bodies integrate it and, thus, become acclimated to it. Second, it is a preparation stage for a deepening.

While this dry spell stage can seem catastrophic to one who has become accustomed (addicted?) to dramatic spiritual experience, the dry spell actually signals a maturing or ripening of sacred experience. If we stay with it, we are weaned of our attachment to the dramatic/ecstatic version of our sacred experience, settling instead into a deepening. In this space, we can let go of any expectations of what sacred experience should be, and let it be what it is: a Re-membering, a homecoming.

3 Homecoming

Step 1, Ecstatic Awakening, is dramatic for a reason: it needs to cut through the multitudinous diversions of the world to attract our attention to the higher things, gearing us toward a conscious shift to alignment with God's plan, with our soul mission and life purpose. But like giving candy to a crying infant, while it serves to distract from the pain, too much can, in some cases, be addictive and, thus, bad for us. It can keep us blocked at that level, moored to ecstatic but less profound experience.

Step 2, the Slowing/Dry Spell, with slowing (or even ceasing) of ecstatic experience can seem terrible if we take it at face value, but there, too, God's Plan is gently prying us from attachment to that beginning phase of our spiritual growth while preparing us for its ripening. The ripening is certain to happen if we stay with it, if we let go of drama, if we accept and open to God's plan.

Step 3, Homecoming, the final step, represents that maturing. We regain connection and fluidity of communication, but without the need for bells and whistles. Our attention to what *is* allows us to Flow with the subtle indicators around us. Angelic and soul accompaniment become as normal for us as human contact, and we are deeply reassured that all is well, that we are loved, that this life is but a (fun) echo of life eternal. It is at this stage that we can most easily help others through the process and impact the world at a different level. This represents The Re-membering, which allows us to align with our soul mission not on our own but in co-creation.

Ahhhhh, living in the world but not of it brings the peace that passeth all understanding! And whether we experience it for a minute, a month, or a year, with every alignment, the homecoming comes more and more easily.

Most people do not experience homecoming or enlightenment in one fell swoop. A sudden and complete opening is possible, but it is rare and often pretty difficult for human vessels to integrate. A more peaceful path brings us again and again into alignment, for longer periods, and more often, until it becomes home on Earth for us. When we have tasted that homecoming, we always want more, so slip-ups can be frustrating. That said, it is perhaps comforting to know that we always go at the rhythm we need to go. It is always best not to force such things. Like a flower that is opening, gentle loving support beats pulling petals open any day! But If we forget that, in those frustrating times, we can ask our Angels to mediate; they are already teamed up with our soul! Or we can even ask our inner child (more on that later).

The exercises in Part Two are designed to bring us into alignment with our soul mission. They worked for me when, after some success heading up the bank's Paris investment banking activity, my job suddenly went away. At that point, I had worked since I was 12 years old—30 years—with 22 of those years in banking. My identity was tied to working, so I definitely felt lost in the vacuum at first. It was an energetic dry spell, unpleasant to experience, but a necessary step for what was to come, as it created space for grace, and for alignment with my soul mission. From that dry spell point, my journey of realignment began. Maybe the exercises that follow will help you or those around you, too.

Part Two

RECOGNIZING THE CALL OF YOUR SOUL— THE RE-MEMBERING

Chapter 5

OPENING THE CHANNEL AND RE-MEMBERING

*I*n the first section of this book, we covered a lot of the eternal aspect of soul mission, providing the context in which we as humans feel a call to meaning and fulfillment, our life purpose. From souls to Angels to Lightworkers to missions and purpose—all of it brought us to the clarity that we, in line with all of creation, experience the sacred rhythm of all that is: expansion and contraction. We emerge from Source, and we return to Source. In between, in our human lives, we experience The Forgetting, and if we are lucky or committed or both, we may also experience The Re-membering while still here on Earth: both the necessary human forgetting as well as the promise of unfolding and Re-membering.

Within that context, using it as a launch pad, we have recognized three steps to spiritual alignment—Ecstatic Awakening, Dry Spell, Homecoming (Re-membering)—and how to recognize when we are aligned: Sweet Spot, Flow, and Familiarity.

Now let us turn our attention (and thus our creative Source energy) to how, step by step, we might bring ourselves into alignment with our soul and our mission. These are precisely the steps I used to do this, and the steps I reuse regularly to keep me on track or help me get back if I feel life has tugged me away from the sweet spot of soul alignment. I have been teaching these steps around the world for many years, with much success. Now, if you are reading this book, these exercises may well help you, too!

The foundational exercises in this book are designed to help you recognize that you are not defined by your instrument (the vessel or body); you

79

are much more. Our human aspect is only our temporary form (physical, emotional, mental, and energetic) expressing the eternal breath of God that is our soul. We operate on the earthly level but also (as soul) at the eternal, spiritual level—the level of Who We Are, Truly.

In order to align with our soul mission and consciously make that alignment our life purpose, it behooves us to open ourselves to the links among these seemingly disparate aspects of our being. In this way, we step into our power and open and embody the bridge between Earth and the heavens we already are; we Re-member. (And why not with the help of the Angels?)

If you have already worked with my book *Inviting Angels into Your Life,* you may already have experienced an exercise similar to this foundational work, since connecting with our heavenly Angels and connecting with our heavenly aspect both require that we, well, connect!

Important Note

If, during any of the exercises in this book, you become woozy or lightheaded, a helpful hint is to open your eyes (if they are closed), even if only slightly. The density of the energy can bring on vertigo, and opening our eyes and allowing in all the stimuli around us disperses or diffuses the energy, easing any symptoms of dizziness. This is in line with the oft-cited universal Law of Energy, "Where our attention goes, so goes the energy."

If you become woozy even if your eyes are open, it is a good idea to gently draw the exercise to a close, no matter where you are in a particular protocol. It is always a good idea to go gently with ourselves, and to remember this important point: Even if we stop, the work is not lost. All energy work functions as a result of our intention. As children of Creator, we create, and "where our attention goes . . ." (Well, you know!) So even if you need to stop, by setting a clear intention at the outset, the work is already effective. The protocol or ritual only serves to reinforce our intention.

Opening the Channel Wide for Re-membering Our Mission

The protocol that follows is not the only way to link our human consciousness with the Divine aspect of our soul, but it is a simple and effective way to go about it with Angelic assistance.

Before getting started, it's important to note that even before we do work like this channel-opening exercise, your channel is already open, at least somewhat. If you are reading this book, you likely have already had "sweet spot" experiences, moments when Earth and Heaven united, which you noticed: Either you felt it (clairsentience), or saw it (clairvoyance), or heard it (clairaudience), or simply knew it (intuition, or claircognizance). Clairvoyant experiences can only occur if our channel between Heaven and Earth is open, at least a little bit. So our intention here will be to deepen our channel, rendering it more fluid.

At sea, a channel is a strait or waterway connecting two bodies of water. Sometimes, as in the case of the Suez Canal (canal is another word for channel), by digging them out, humans make channels more fluid, and thus, more useful. Similarly, the more often we use our channel (by doing this or similar exercises, for example), the more we "dig it out," rendering more fluid our lines of communication between Earth and Sky. As with physical water channels, this "digging out" facilitates connectivity and communication between us in our human material form and Source in all heavenly expression, including as our soul and heavenly allies like the Angels.

 Exercise

PROTOCOL FOR OPENING THE CHANNEL

1 Breathe to prepare

When you decide to do this, to open your channel wider, farther, it is important to choose a quiet space away from curious eyes, a place where you won't be interrupted. The exercise can be done in any position, but it is best not to try it lying down, especially in the beginning, unless absolutely necessary.

Close your eyes and . . . breathe!

Although we breathe about 10,000 times a day, most of the time it is unconscious. Our work here is to render our mission conscious (and thus, attainable), so we will want to breathe consciously here.

We know that breath carries life, our human experience beginning with the first breath of a baby, and ending with our last breath at death, when Life is carried on our breath, on to our next adventure. Knowing this, we can imagine that conscious breathing in itself is an exercise that can enliven our life, putting our soul mission at breath's reach!

To that end, *breathe in* life, and *breathe out* anything that has been distracting you or weighing on you, diminishing your life, your Light, your Joy, your shine! Repeat until you begin to feel clearer and lighter.

2 Set your intention

Once you feel ready, *breathe in* your intention to open your instrument to your Divine gifts and Angelic assistance, and *breathe out* anything outside of that intention that might distract you. Breathe in that intention until you feel it fill you in the moment, with no distractions whatsoever. Remember, breath centers us in life, our life in this moment, the only time that intention work such as this channel opening is possible. Stay present!

3 Ask your Angels for help

If you would like to have some heavenly help with this channel opening, why not ask your Angels for help? No matter if you don't know anything about them or are not even sure they exist (yet). They do not need you to believe in them to assist you (besides that is how most of us come to really believe in them, as they show or "prove" themselves to us). They only need you to ask, so that the free will requirement is met.

How to ask them? Keep it simple, sweetie! Your words, spoken from the heart, are always perfect; speak whatever comes from your heart. It can be a prayer that you have always felt drawn to, or something simple like, *Hi, Angels. I intend to open my channel to communicate with you (more clearly). Please help in this. Thank you!* (It is always good to include both a clear intention and a word of thanks; gratitude is an energy of high frequency and facilitates things.)

4 Fill your body with Light

Imagine or see or feel or know that with each breath you breathe in, you breathe in Light, the Light of your soul, of your mission.

As you breathe in, send that Light down to the tips of your toes and fingers, lighting up each cell, and even the spaces between the cells. Continuing, you will bring more and more Light into the body, and each out-breath will clear out any shadow that has blocked your Light, any shadow that can be released at this time, will be released.

In: Light!

Out: Anything that blocks your Light (with the help of the Angels).

Continue until you feel ready for the next step.

5 Light up your spinal column

Continue to breathe in Light, but on the out-breath, use a sweeping breath to send that Light to your spinal column. See, feel, sense, or simply know that you are lighting it up from your neck down to your coccyx.

This path of Light illuminates your spinal column, which physically and energetically represents that you are the bridge between Earth and Sky. It will form the base of your channel, as you are creating (or reinforcing) it with intention today, with the help of your Angels.

6 Connect with the earth

When the spine is alight with clear intention send forth your path of Light, from the coccyx down into the center of the earth. See or feel or know or imagine that the beam of Light easily makes its way down to the center of the earth, with the earth itself opening to welcome you, layer by layer, opening and supporting your journey of Light, all the way to the center of our Mother Earth, the heart of the planet.

The welcome is warming, rich and nourishing. *Breathe In* the strength and power that is here, and *breathe out* all that might have until now blocked your power, your ability to live in the "sweet spot," in alignment with your soul mission.

When you are ready, notice or simply know that you are not alone; that the consciousness of Mother Earth is present, as if she has been waiting all along! Seeing you arrive, she holds out her arms to give you a great hug, pulling you close to her heart, like a good mother who has missed her child. This is perfectly normal, as truly, the moment you as a soul chose to take on the flesh and blood of mortal existence, you became her child. She is mother to all beings that express physically on Earth.

Let this good mother fill you with tenderness and Love. Take a moment to receive this Love, you who give so much to the world. She knows well all that you have had to face in this life, how difficult it has sometimes been, and she is aware of the importance of your soul mission, your life purpose.

She intends to fill you with every strength and skill you will require to fulfill your mission. Will you accept it? Will you open now your channel to receive this reinforcing energetic boost from Mother Earth? (Your free will precludes this happening without your accord.)

Just say yes!

Accepting her offering is easy. Simply set the intention to open to the help and support of Earth, to the true strength and power of your instrument, to your unique expression of Light in this lifetime. Your own words from the heart are always best, but it can be something simple like:

I open my channel to stand strong upon the earth, grounded and ready to live my soul mission. Thank you, Mother. Thank you, Source.

You may then see or feel or simply know the end of your beam of Light is now rooted here at the center of the earth. The channel between your human form and the earth is in place!

Before moving on to the next step, *breathe in* the love, tenderness, strengthening, and confidence-building on offer from the earth. *Breathe out* anything that has shaken your strength and confidence, and perhaps at times your will to live on this planet! Continue breathing and fill your whole body (instrument) and prepare for the next step.

7 Fill the body with earth energy

Thanking Mother Earth for her generous filling energy, and maybe offering her a kiss on the cheek and a quick "See you later!" (we will), it is time to take your leave of her, to move back to and up through your channel, which is now strongly rooted in the earth, the beam of light that stretches already (because you have opened it) between the earth and you.

Go up. This happens easily with your intention, and as you rise, your movement is supported by a powerful flow of energy following you and then carrying you. The nourishing energy of Mother Earth flows forcefully, lifting and carrying you upward, as if on a geyser, up and up.

Again, the layers of the earth pass easily by as you travel with help to return whence you began: through the earth, through the foundation of any structure where you now are, into your body, and up your brilliantly lit spinal column, all the way to your heart.

The heart is the lynchpin connecting Earth and Sky, the seat of our inner knowing, which comes from soul and expresses through our humanity. For this reason, it is a good idea to take a moment here to integrate the earth strengthening and rooting before continuing.

Arriving at the level of your heart, take a moment to let that strength of Love and tenderness fill your thirsting being and your heart to overflowing, then your whole physical body, your mental and emotional bodies, and finally, your energy field, your spiritual body.

Allow the filling until your whole being is full of Light, not just your spinal column. When this is the case, your deep-rooted connection with the earth is in place, and the filling and grounding of your instrument has readied you for the next step: a stable foundation that will support the second opening to occur.

8 Connecting to the Angels

When you feel full, set your sights (and intention) on the heavens! From the level of your heart, follow your beam of light channel up the spinal column, through the neck, the head, and out the crown chakra (situated at the fontanelle, between the frontal and parietal bones on top of the head, the last place a skull hardens in a human). Use your intention to voyage forth to the heavens, to Source/God, to your soul, your Angels, to all allies at the highest level.

Happy for the invitation, the Angels around you accompany your journey. Let yourself be carried to the heavens on Angel wings. Lifted up and up and up, and then arriving, you may feel an expansion or lightheadedness. (Remember: if it is too much, simply open your eyes again.) *Breathe in* the Light and Love and Joy of the Source. *Breathe out* anything that in the past may have clouded your Joy, your Light, your Re-membering, your mission!

Of course, the Angels welcome you home, for indeed, this is your true home; here, you are known and loved. Here, at Source, your soul dwells eternally, that part of you that never believed itself separate from God. Here, in this space, you can easily cultivate connection with Angels and Archangels, your Guides and Ascended Masters, as your soul already has these connections in unity. Today, we are here to align with soul and to access Angelic help in so doing.

Are you ready to open to your soul and accept your soul mission as your chosen life purpose? If so, this is best facilitated by opening your channel to your soul and Source now. In your own words, set your intention to complete the opening of your channel to the highest planes of being, Re-membering with your soul. Something simple and heartfelt is always best, maybe something like this:

> *I am ready and willing to open to the Light and Love and Joy of the Divine, and so, to my Light and Love and Joy. I do this now by aligning myself consciously with my true self, the soul. I invite my soul to fully incarnate through me, and make of the soul's mission, my human, conscious life purpose.*
>
> *In this, I ask the help of my Angels from this moment forward, especially the Guardian Presence of God around me, Archangel Michael, and _____ (insert the Archangels, if any, to whom you felt called in Chapter 3).*

With your words, you may notice or feel or know that the beam of your channel of Light seems to anchor here at Source. But whether you feel it or not, it is so; your intention is that powerful! We are children of Creation/Creator, and we create all the time, unconsciously or consciously. (Consciously is more powerful, or course.) Our conscious expectations and intentions create in almost as solid a manner as our physical actions: "Where our attention goes, so goes our energy" that creates.

Wide open, connected to soul, with your Angels around you now, *breathe in*, and notice how it feels as you are filled. Allow the Light and Love to fill you, the Joy to overflow. *Breathe out* anything that comes up in mind or heart to distract or block this.

Keep *breathing in* that Light and *breathing out*, releasing any blocks to your Light, to your soul Re-membering, to your mission. When you are full, feel or sense or know that you are now revitalized, and you are ready for anything!

9 Return and integrate

When you have had your fill and are ready to complete, ask your soul and your Angels to accompany you henceforth, and they will! Enjoy their Presence, as they accompany your descent along your channel/beam of Light, returning entirely to the Earth plane and your physical dimension. Slide along this path you have created (which will become wider and more fluid with each use) to return to the physical body.

In good company, come back into the space where you are, and follow down into the body through your head, neck, and upper spinal column until you reach the level of your heart. At the heart, place your hands at the center of your chest (where the heart chakra is located).

Breathe in to bring your consciousness to your heart beating within your chest, poised between Earth and Sky. Know that you are on your way, that any doors that had been closed are now reopening, your energetic Re-membering and realignment with your soul with the help of the Angels is well on its way. Gratitude!

Why Aftercare Is Necessary

After such an exercise, you may feel tired. Rest, if possible. The physical body, particularly if we are not used to energy work, may be easily fatigued by working with our channel, especially at first. But that changes quickly when we apply ourselves!

That said, it is a very good idea to care for our instrument (like a master violinist might care for his Stradivarius after playing it) each and every time we reach out energetically to our soul and to the Angels for help and healing, aligning to mission.

When we do an exercise like the channel opening we just experienced, we expand energetically: our energy field becomes bigger and more powerful. Such an exercise aligns us with our soul (and thus, our mission) more each time. However, our physical body can be slow to adjust; it is always aligned with the energetic footprint we had before the exercise, so it will try to attune with our new energetic footprint. The frequency of our cells rise, which may in the moment tire our physical vessel.

How Can We Help?

Here are some things you can do to assist your body in adapting to the "new you":

- *Drink water.* This helps with the evacuation of anything that no longer serves, and helps the instrument, which is mostly made of water, to acclimate to your new, expanded energy footprint.

- *Go for a walk (or sit) in Nature.* This helps you ground further and integrate the work. Do this barefoot, if possible.
- *Eat nuts or fresh fruit.* Organic is preferable, and/or blessed.
- *Sing or chant.* The vibration facilitates the integration.
- *Relax.* When we are asleep, soul takes over, and integration is facilitated. Take a nap, sleep, or even daydream. Find the rest necessary for integration.

Of course, this list is not exhaustive. These are only a few of the organic, simple techniques to integrate expansions along the way to living our soul mission with the help of the Angelic realm. But they are a good place to start!

Chapter 6

OBSTACLES ON THE PATH
AND THEIR RESOLUTION

*I*n Part One, we set the table with understandings about the rules of the game of Life, and now, through the work of the last chapter, we have opened ourselves up energetically to align with our soul and Source, our highest mission and purpose. We have seen that we already have experienced moments of alignment with that Highest, through recognizing the synchronicity of Flow situations and the wonderful sweet-spot experiences we may have had from time to time, leading up to right now.

But (since we are human and living on Earth in duality), it is likely that we have also experienced the opposite of the sweet spot: times when we feel like we might be in the type of spiritual dry spell we spoke of earlier, or worse, times when we *know* we are stuck!

At such times, nothing flows, and Life is a struggle. We are swimming upstream, and nothing comes easily. Bad things do happen—yes, even to good people. In fact, this has nothing to do with "bad" or "good," and certainly is not a question of deserving or not deserving. There is no cosmic judge punishing us midstream (or afterward, for that matter) on our journey.

Rather, these experiences when life feels like an obstacle course are *also* meant to serve, to drive us to a shift in direction, to awakening and Re-membering. Such difficult periods always mark a time when we have forgotten (or are in denial of) Who We Are, Truly; thus, the path that is ours becomes like an obstacle path, and energetically we may even feel as if we are being pulled downward into a hole where we can't see clearly.

But how is it possible to fall into such a hole when we have already experienced the sweet spot of being aligned with soul and Source? And what do we do to get out of that hole, if life events bring us back there from time to time? How can we recognize and avoid—or failing that, climb out of—pitfalls on the path?

Pitfalls on the Path

Before we get into the work of sorting out our individual purposes and next steps, it is helpful to know where the pitfalls on the path might be, and how to avoid or transform them.

Pitfalls that are conscious or unconscious can come from within us or from without. They can make it feel like someone is conspiring against us, even while our Angelic and soul team is bringing support and Love. Such pitfalls include *fear of the unknown, temptation and distractions, pressure from loved ones, not wanting to hurt others, our reputation (what others think of us),* and *self-judgment* or lack of self-esteem, thinking we don't deserve the good that awaits us.

Each of these pitfalls blocks our flow and kills our access to our sweet spot, and each one is remedied first by understanding that it is happening, and why. Shining the light of consciousness on these obstacles to Flow is a necessary step before we look to create a step-by-step plan for our sweet spot, for Joy!

Fear of the Unknown

One of the most pervasive blocks to our alignment with soul and mission (and thus, Joy!) is a fear of the unknown that we basically inherited. This is not "ours," and we didn't choose this fear; rather, we have been breathing it in since our arrival on the planet. Human beings fear the unknown on a rudimentary, animal level, connected to the part of the brain known as the amygdala, in conjunction with other brain functions.

People largely prefer the known (even the unpleasant) to the unknown, and for many of us, a situation has to devolve to the really unpleasant, or even beyond that which we can stand, before we will opt for change. Change, especially when we are not choosing to be okay with it, is difficult. Status quo is our comfort zone, our blanket fort (where nothing grows).

The brain's cortex compares everything we come upon in life to what we have already experienced, to determine if the fight-or-flight response is needed. When an experience does not match anything in our experience repertoire, the default position is danger and flight-or-fight is triggered.

Pondering changes, even changes to align us with a sweet spot life of Flow and magic, can trigger a chain reaction in the brain, resulting in a flight-or-fight response, including physical sensations, from dramatically increased pulse/heart rate to too-quick shallow breathing. The body tenses, we become alert, and our bloodstream is flooded with adrenaline, supporting the possibility of fast, defensive, instinctive action (fight-or-flight).

This part of our (human) being was designed to protect the instrument in case of mortal danger, but in a world where most of us face arguably fewer of those (no more velociraptors), the mechanism has been misappropriated unconsciously (depending on our vessel and our beginning environment) to react in the same aggressive way in the face of even small changes.

We all know, don't we, someone who massively overreacts to anything or everything? Perhaps they yell, scream, or punch (fight), or they don't show up, abruptly go silent, or cut off all contact (flight)? Eventually, once calm again prevails, they might sheepishly apologize, or worse, act as if nothing happened.

These reactions are always fear expressing. They can be either related to fear of failure or fear of success, but they are what keep many of us in our blanket forts, instead of going out in the world to play our soul's chosen role.

So how do we transform such a pitfall? Why not ask the Angels to help? And look at the following possible solutions.

Solution: Slow down

It is great if, even to some degree, we recognize this pattern within us, as that will help us to release it and lead the kind of aligned life that will bring no regrets at the end. The key is to recognize the pattern. When we see or feel or know any of the reactions noted above going on in our physical body, any dis-ease or discomfort with a particular situation, notice it, and do nothing! Just breathe. Notice it, and just breathe. That's it.

In this way, we allow our body to process the fear that has arisen, giving ourselves the chance to digest it and calm down without blocking anything, and without fighting or fleeing. In line with the universal law "As within, so without," as we relax our body with breath, we allow Flow within, leading us to allow Flow without.

Slowing down in this way in the face of fear of the unknown keeps doors open and helps us to avoid doing or saying anything we might regret later. In this way, we take the time to understand that we are fearful not because there is something to fear, but because most of us are conditioned to be fearful of anything we have never experienced, of what we cannot control, the unknown.

Love/Trust

Fear is the opposite of Love, thus, when we are triggered in the face of the unknown and fear floods our body, we are pushed into reaction, and this blocks our access to Love and experiences of Love flowing toward our mission. In fact, like two sides of the same coin, this is Earth's duality in action: heads or tails; fear or Love. Both at the same time are not possible.

If we stay in fear of the unknown, we swim upstream, refusing what is, but what is arising always leads us farther toward our mission, our Re-membering. Fear will always block it, and we may find we are either fighting or fleeing what we know is in our best interests.

But if we slow down when faced with new circumstances, we can slowly shift the blockage by actually loving the new, or at least allowing ourselves to have a healthy curiosity toward it, recognizing it as a gift from the heavens. Nothing is by chance, and every experience, "negative" or "positive," is a door opening to bring us farther along.

With such practice, we can really let go of the fear the world trained us to have, and by loving the obstacle, the blockage will be transformed into an asset.

Temptation

We spoke earlier about Christ energy, the highest frequency of Light and Love, of God. Walking our path toward our mission always brings us toward Christ energy, alignment with Heaven's will. But since when we stretch toward Light, darkness responds, and this may (save for the grace of God, when it would not serve) lead us to temptation and distraction.

In my experience, when we set our sights higher (envisioning a goal, perhaps), the Universe steps up to test our resolve. For example, we may decide to stay away from a person who impacts us negatively, and then get a message from that person immediately after we decide. Or we may decide to do a fast, and then a friend drops by with a cake. These seeming coincidences are not coincidences at all, but experiences that provide us with a context to strengthen our intention, if we stick with our good intention, or not. (I stayed away from the person but ate the banana bread!)

This is not to say that we should judge ourselves; being tempted and sometimes falling is part of a human journey here on Earth, and guilt is worse than failing! Guilt is a huge distraction from our Light, and a lower energy than fear (we will see this later). Falling does not matter; it is how and when and why we get up again that will strengthen our movement along the path to our soul's mission.

But don't take my (banana bread) word for it. The Master called Jesus Christ was tempted, and the details are included in the Bible. If we look at Matthew 4:1-11, we see Jesus tempted in three ways: by bread, by protection, and by power. It may be that we recognize these temptations in other forms.

Bread

Jesus was fasting in the wilderness for 40 days, and, as he was human, was hungry. Satan tempted Jesus, trying to distract Him from the mission, saying that he only needed to turn a stone into bread and be satiated. Jesus said no, with the famous response, "Man cannot live on bread alone, but by every word from the mouth of God."

Think of how this might play out in modern life. Ever hear (or say) anything like this? "Don't try to be an artist, dear. You will starve." Or "Do something practical. Grow up!" Or "You can create art on the side if you must, but you need to earn a living, put a roof over your head!" Or "I am not paying for college unless you study to be a doctor. Forget about music!"

In a world that has some very clear (and limiting) beliefs about what one should do to live (that is, to "earn a living"), many have been convinced to turn away from their heart's desire and their highest path, buying instead what the world is selling: a false sense of protection.

Fortunately, this paradigm is shifting, but bucking the system to pursue our dreams is still not always easy, but always worth it!

In a world where even "stable and safe" jobs are no longer ensured, following our hearts to soul choice is a more plausible path than ever. And the soul, Source, makes no mistakes. Foregoing rich Life in order to simply exist was never the plan. If we have a desire in our heart, that desire was seeded by soul and Source, and we have the power to choose it, and realize it.

Safety

In the same Biblical passage, Satan tempted Jesus to throw himself from a cliff and call the Angels to protect him. The response was another famous line, "Thou shalt not put the Lord thy God to the test." How does this play out for Lightworkers of today?

The key here is that Satan was tempting Jesus with the idea of safety. In our society today, the idea of safety goes right along with the idea of bread, doesn't it? The idea of safety expands from having enough to eat and a roof over our head, to feeling safe, sheltered against risks of violence and poverty. The world says that we are safe when we have enough money in the bank, when we have health insurance, when our worldly needs are met, but is it true?

Here on Earth, are we ever free from risk? Even if we are hiding out in our blanket fort, are we safe? Couldn't there be an earthquake, a flood, a fire? (Maybe why so many of them are happening these days, forcing many back into the game?)

We did not come into the game of Life to hide from Life. But when we do hide, when we resist the Flow to our sweet spot, we are resisting God's invitation, God's will. Of course, we are allowed to do that as long as we like (free will in action), but if we remain in hiding, not sharing our gifts with the world, it is likely that our soul is going to give us a nudge, maybe by sending an Angel into a bank with a crystal!

Power

The last form of temptation that Jesus withstood, as described in Matthew 1, was power. Satan took Jesus up to the heights and offered him dominion over all of it, if only Jesus would bow down. Jesus of course said no, exclaiming: "Go, Satan! For it is written, 'Ye shall worship the Lord thy God and serve Him only.' Then the devil left Him, and behold, Angels came and began to minister to Him." Can we see how this might apply to modern life?

The path to the Highest is not about wielding earthly power but wielding the power of who we are truly. It is not about worldly recognition but alignment with Love, with the Highest. That said, there are of course cases where people who sense a calling to a spiritual life, choose instead a life inclined toward the world's ambitions of money and power. Such choices are never "forever"; we are always given the possibility to reconsider. (After 22 years in international banking, my soul breathed a sigh of relief when I made another choice.)

In everyday terms, the pitfall of temptation of power often takes the form of choosing what will attract worldly esteem and power over spiritual power, ignoring the soul's call to answer the call of worldly life and living according to the world's values.

Yet even on a spiritual path, the temptation of worldly power, especially if it is unconscious, can be a great obstacle to mission, and can take on many forms. If this obstacle were expressed as a conscious choice of power above the soul's mission service to God/Love, a person might become an energetic "vampire," drawing out energy, power, and money from others to feed their needs. Such "gurus" attract soul contract beings, but their work cannot go much farther. When people go into spiritual work for money, it often does not work, and they eventually learn that lesson.

But sometimes, people are unconscious in their attempts to attract power to them. With very good intentions, they might believe their heart is in the right place, not noticing the ups and downs of their ego being fed or not. In such cases, we can imagine that the inner child is still hungry for affection, and that information can help us, as we will see later, transform this blockage into a strong point.

In healing practices, this is very important to note. Some practitioners (no matter what the modality) believe that if a healing occurs, they "did" it; they healed the person. The truth is, no healing can happen if the soul underlying the human receiving the healing session does not allow that healing. In truth, *all we practitioners do is create a space of healing in which the person self-heals.* When we see and know this is true, much of the temptation to power falls away. This is great news! That means that we do not get the "credit," but also do not carry the burden of the person's healing. Our only job is to ensure that our channel is as clear and fluid as possible.

Solution: Slow and Fill

For each of these temptations, it is important to shine the light of consciousness on it in order to transform it. The recurring theme here will be to go sufficiently slowly and pay sufficient attention to what is going on in both our outer and inner landscapes, in order to choose wisely and avoid or transform the temptations noted. Once we have been going slowly enough to notice that temptation is blocking us, a key is to recognize what is missing and fill it ourselves. If we are scared and, thus, tempted by money, quietly and calmly taking a look at what our true material needs are and how we can fill them clears away the panicky haze of fear.

If we are scared about not being safe, recognizing that we are in a world where there is no such thing as safety (not even hiding out under the covers, which is not Life at all), we can accompany that part of us who is scared, holding ourselves by the hand with loving reassurance. (We will do this in the next section on the Inner Child.) If we are tempted by power, examining where we have felt powerless in our lives and accessing the power that is anchored deep within in alignment with Who We Are, Truly (our soul) will fill the need within. (Why not ask for help from the all-powerful and loving Angels of God?)

Pressure from Loved Ones

When we love someone, we give them a special place in our heart, and their opinions, wants, and desires will most often carry more weight than those of others. Pressure from loved ones can lead us to postpone or give up our soul mission, our sweet spot; we may even believe that doing so is selfless and for the highest good, which is most often not true, as we will explore here. This blockage to our alignment with soul mission is related to the fear of the unknown and temptations noted above. The pressure we receive from loved ones is often the overflow of their own fear of the unknown and the instability of Life when we change (remember the canoe?).

These fears can be easily linked to the three temptations noted above: *bread, security,* and *power.*

Bread

Sometimes our loved ones are just worried about where the bread—the money—will come from if we change in accordance with our soul mission. I personally can say that when the bank I was working for shifted strategy in Europe, and my job in Paris went away and I rejected the other jobs that were offered to replace it, my then-husband was not delighted. We lived in a nice part of town in a beautiful apartment, and had lots of money for travel and fun. Who could blame him?

When we can't see the higher picture, it is difficult to have faith that things are unfolding as they are meant to; that is, for the best. For our loved ones, especially if they are impacted by our choices financially, this can be very trying, even creating an existential panic or fear if they have been comfortable or hiding under the covers. Many people are not at all prepared for change, so it is important to have compassion for them, even as we transform the blockage.

Security

For our loved ones, our movement to change can trigger fears around security, ours or theirs. For example, a friend or relative who is an excellent retirement specialist might express concern that we seem to be unconcerned by retirement. Or a person with whom we live might worry about homelessness, as temptations that limit us will often tend toward the dramatic.

It is important to remember here that the fears are often exaggerated to panic, and that energy will pull us away from Flow. As an ex-banker, I am the last person to tell others to ignore retirement planning or budget on a day-to-day basis. The key is balance: to reassure the human beings around us (loved ones, as well as ourselves) that we are still very much taking care of business, even while shifting to a Flow-based Life movement in alignment with soul. Once they see the fruit of our sweet-spot Flow, pressure will ease!

Power

Lastly, we might receive pressure from those around us who are used to having power over us. In any relationship (family, friend, lover), there is a balance of power that may swing this way or that, depending on what is going on. However, there is sometimes an imbalance of power that allows one partner to bully the other, subtly through manipulation or less subtly, by physical or emotional force or emotional blackmail. While the former is obvious, the latter might be less obvious. When a person pushes us to act against our own well-being by emotional bribery or guilt-tripping, this manipulation is a power play. In such cases it is always a good idea to take our power back!

When we are in such a situation, it is always a soul contract, and both sides have something to learn. Taking our power back in such a situation reinforces our flow in line with our soul mission and creates a context for change in our power-hungry partners. Though this shift in paradigm might be difficult to swallow for the other person, freeing the relationship from this highly-charged imbalance is always for the best for all concerned!

Not Wanting to Hurt Others

This blockage to our Flow is obviously related to "Pressure from Others," above, but in this case, the loved one is not pressuring us to do anything; instead, we pressure ourselves!

Such pressure we might place on ourselves can be based on limiting beliefs about our loved ones, possibly the false, egoic idea that the other person can't handle our truth, our shifting. Sometimes, this obstacle may be covering up a personal fear of the unknown/fear of failure.

They Can't Handle It

If we are putting pressure on ourselves to not go forward so as to not hurt others, we may unconsciously be carrying limiting beliefs about our loved ones, maybe related to the three temptations: bread, safety, or power.

- *Bread.* We may believe that the person cannot support themselves financially, and so (martyred) we cannot change.
- *Safety.* We may believe that the person cannot protect themselves, and so (again martyred) we cannot change.
- *Power.* We may believe that the person needs us to live, that it is our power that sustains them.

Obviously, any of these three points are egoic temptations. If we believe things like this, it feeds the ego—the ego that doesn't really want to align with/be dissolved into soul! We may be reluctant to speak our truth, thinking that our loved one cannot handle it. This implicitly reveals that we believe we are bigger and more powerful than the other.

Solution

Recognize that any such intricate deep relationships are always soul contracts, and know that this is coming up for healing at this time. The truth is that on a soul level you have decided to engage with this person in exactly this way, and you have free will with regard to how you choose to respond: either through fear or Love.

- *The View of Love.* Let the worrying about the question rest. If we are meant to stay with someone, it will be our "sweet spot" to do so. We will want to journey with them, and they, with us. That journeying together will bring us into alignment with our highest soul missions, even if it isn't easy.
- *The View of Fear.* Even if our path is calling us elsewhere, we may choose to ignore that truth but perhaps hide under the covers in a

relationship blanket fort. This is not fair to the other person, who deserves a friend or partner (in business or in life) who loves to walk with them, and hiding is not conducive to living the mission we have come to express. Releasing fear in this case will allow more space for grace and Love for all concerned.

What Others Think about Us

Sometimes what blocks our flowing to mission is about a more subtle pressure pushing us to be like others. The longing to belong is strong in humans, and so we often want to be part of groups. Swimming upstream is always tough, and often our soul will call us away from the beaten path to our unique expression of Source. Which is great . . . except when it's not.

Huh?

Well, how many times have you chosen differently from those around you and been celebrated for it?

When we step out of line, most often we see (non-congratulatory) responses ranging from something like, "Really? Hmmm . . ." to "Do you think that is a good idea?" to "Seriously, girl, you need to have your head examined!" to (my personal favorite) "I liked her better when she was a drunk."

As we discussed earlier, people don't like it when we step out of line, but also, *we* don't like it when we step out of line and are rejected or excluded or judged as a result of our "sweet spot" choices.

In the (highly likely) event that following our dreams will bring us success (perhaps not in terms of worldly values but a deeper, richer sense of fulfillment, or both), many (not all) people will pretend not to notice, or begrudgingly utter some words of congratulations, all the while incredulous that it should happen to us (not seeing that our courage *attracted* the marvel). But before that happens, when it is only taking courage to buck a system with only unknown and unknowable terrain behind the curtain we are choosing, the opinion of the world can present a block to our human being longing to fit in.

Solution: Slow and Fill

Again, slowing down here can help, as well as feeling the emotions that are there: the need for Love and acceptance. As ever, it is then important to accompany ourselves on our path, filling our need for Love and acceptance ourselves. (We will explore this shortly.) In this way, we address the need at the root, within, instead of waiting for the approval of others, without. The best thing about letting go of the need for approval from others is that often once we let go of it, we get it! People are excited by and curious about and admiring of folks who are confident in themselves. Self-love attracts loving selves!

Self-Judgment

The last blockage to life purpose Flow that the Angels want us to look out for here is perhaps the most generally damaging: self-judgment. Specifically, when we have (unconsciously or consciously) decided that we are not worthy of the Highest, that we don't deserve to live in the sweet spot of alignment. Self-judgment or self-loathing, a lack of self-love, is a significant impediment to progress and to our shining!

To surpass this obstacle, we need to first understand where it comes from and then proceed to soften and transform it.

We come from Source, so at some point before we were born, at the beginning of Life, we knew we were good, an expression of God, even, as demonstrated by our being here on Earth, part of God's work (G.O.D.—Good Orderly Direction). So what happened?

For many of us (not all), our landing on Earth brought us into contact with lower energies than our own, and as we know, energy seeks equilibrium! For this reason, shining, Light-filled, unique children are often bullied and berated by other children and adults whose frequencies are lower. When a light is too bright, what do we do? We dim it or shut it off! Similarly, if we outshine, if we are not in phase with others, they will say or do things in a (conscious or unconscious) effort to dim our shine. With time, maybe we even learn to dim our own shine in their presence in order to fit in and avoid unpleasant experiences.

In this way, over years of hiding our Light (the danger of those comfortable blanket forts!), we run the risk of forgetting our Light completely: in so doing, we lose touch with our Joy. Our Light is our Joy, an expression of God's Love.

Sometimes, we see the Light in a child's eyes; other times, sadly, it may seem like that Light has gone out. Depending on our initial context, where we were born, and how our vessels were set out in the waters of Life, we may have hidden our Light, even as a child, in an effort to preserve it, or it may feel like it has dimmed or even gone out. In any case, when our Light is hidden and thus, inaccessible to us, we may have been impacted by lower energies leading us to speak and think and take action not at all in line with our highest expression. This can create regret or guilt and pull us even farther away from our soul Light.

It is important to note that the limiting beliefs that we are not good enough, or that we are undeserving, or untalented or unloved *don't belong to us;* they belong to a world that tries to keep everyone in line, a world that understands precious little of the magic that awaits us on this God-blessed voyage of Life.

Solution

Once we can see clearly that there is a dearth of self-esteem or self-love to transform, we can begin the work of the next section, reaching out to our inner child and recovering and boosting our light and Joy, in alignment with our soul mission.

Chapter 7
THE INNER CHILD RE-MEMBERS

Truly I tell you, unless you change and become like little children, you will never enter the kingdom of heaven.

Matthew 18:3, The Bible

*J*esus's words are really the key to what we are doing here. If we imagine that He was speaking to absolute truths and not temporal ones, Christ was not asking us to behave in childish ways, but reminding us to Re-member Who We Are, Truly: eternally innocent and Joyful beings who are always in the sweet spot He called the Kingdom of Heaven.

We are reminded that within us is an aspect that always remains connected to Source; a part of us that *knows* that God holds us in the palm of His hand; a part of us that would dearly love to relax fully in God's Love, with the trust and confidence of a well-loved child.

We know what that confidence is, don't we? We can tell—see, sense, feel, or know—the difference between a child who is well-loved and one who is not, can't we? Whether we have experienced this personally or not, doesn't the well-loved child shine, while the light of the other is somehow clouded? Doesn't the well-loved child have the daring of bold laughter and expecting to be seen and admired, while the other child seems to try to hide in a corner?

While almost everyone delights in the shenanigans of the well-loved child, we might want to shout (like in the now-classic film *Dirty Dancing*), "Nobody puts Baby in the corner!" when we see the light already dimming in the eyes of the less-loved child, too-young eyes that have already seen too much ugliness in the world.

Now, imagine these two extreme but common cases all grown up. Which one do you think will be more likely to dare to speak their Truth and live their sweet spot mission? Which one maybe not so much? Exactly!

So many obstacles to our mission of Re-membering are rooted in limiting beliefs cultivated by early experience in our lives. Knowing that we are loved breeds confidence, and true confidence is marked by being able to breathe deeply, by being able to relax; knowing that all is well—that we have enough bread, safety, and power, for example. If we didn't have enough bread or safety or power (or Love) early in our lives, we may have started out "behind the eight ball" (that is, unlucky) in terms of our mission, or if the voyage of Life brought us lack of Love, bread, safety, or power, we may have been on track but feel like we lost it along the way.

If that is the case, how do we get back to the sweet spot, find our mojo, Re-member, when low energies in the world have pulled us away?

There is one sure-fire way to get our mojo back: we open up to that space within us that never left the Garden, that is aware of God's love at all times, that Light that maybe we hid or that got dimmed. It is time to fan the flame, bringing the Light of consciousness to our fumbling in the dark! And why not, with help from the Angels, channel open, and accompanied by our Friends in High Places? Remembering that the child we came in as, ever pure and innocent, holds the key to the Kingdom of Heaven, our soul mission and Flow will be the answer.

In this chapter we will first reestablish or strengthen our connection to that deep aspect of ourselves (the inner-child Light) that perhaps has been shaken or gone into hiding because of the harshness of the world.

Where I grew up, the Bronx of the Seventies and Eighties was a tough place. Some considered it normal, but I lost several friends to violence very young, and home was no safe haven. Later, life on Wall Street reinforced the idea that only the tough survive, and so, my experience forced me to hide the soft part of me that just wanted to love and be loved. I did my faux-tough act for many years; for that time, it was my blanket fort, and I hoped like hell it would protect me. It didn't. Though I survived those times, I did not come out unscathed; in fact, exceedingly scathed! That is why I did not know how to welcome the gift of that crystal in the bank that magical day.

As we move into adulthood, the world encourages us to put away, hide, squelch, or even lose our tenderness. We are taught that what is invisible does not exist, and are encouraged to set aside intuition for facts and Angels for accountancy ledgers. The voyage to adulthood thus takes us farther and farther away from our sweet spot, and away from the child we once were who had easier access to Joy and our soul mission.

The world urges (or forces) us to toughen up in order to protect ourselves, and most of us do just that from the beginning, imagining that hardness will provide the safety we desire. It is a lie and sadly, a trick of pandemic proportions.

The True Pandemic—Shuttered Heart Syndrome

Imagine that we emerge into this world from pure Love, from Source (we do). When we land on Earth, our original tendency will thus be to, well, love, *non?* Of course, it is! Now imagine a child who is pure Love shining forth, arms akimbo and ready to love the whole wide world, shouting, "Look at meeeeeeee!!!"

Even in the best of families, the infinite and unconditional Love of Source is not replicated. Humans put conditions on things, and if we are fortunate enough to land in a family that knows how to love, is it ever 24/7, constant, at every moment? Nope! Humans get tired (and loving can be tiring when it is conditional).

So when a child arrives on the scene, heart wide open and ready to love BIG, often there is an adjustment that takes place, a stepping back, a muting of that Love, so that it can take on a form that will be welcomed and appreciated.

In nurturing families, this adjustment may be small, but we learn when to go hug Mom, and when not to; when to approach Dad, and when to duck him, depending on his mood, and so on. In a family that is not nurturing, scary even, other learnings occur. We might learn how to disappear altogether, if need be. As we grow up, these learnings continue, as teacher and boss replace Mom and Dad. Warily, we tread the path we first set out on, and rarely do we diverge from it into unknown terrain, not if we can help it!

From the beginning, then, when we land on Earth, there is a light adjustment that occurs. Since we know that energy seeks equilibrium, it is not surprising that the world dims our Light at the outset, forcing us to shut down our hearts, if only a little.

The world is heading for a change, though. You know this, don't you? It has already begun, and your personal and individual quest to align with your soul mission is part of it! The Angels are at the ready, hoping to be asked to help remedy the pandemic of shut-down hearts. If we keep our hearts shut, or selectively open, we will never be fully in our sweet spot, because we will never fully be ourselves. The Angels invite us to throw caution to the wind and go for the Re-membering, the reopening of our hearts, with the clarity that this will be the remedy that will help the earth.

When our hearts are open, we are not defended. But we cannot force our hearts to open; the habitual spring-locks are set, and it may take time to release them before we can live our soul contract fully, relaxing into our sweet spot, and unleashing the power (Source) that is our heart.

In order to do that, what was done must be undone. We must create the context that will allow us to relax and know that all is well. By loving and protecting ourselves, that tender part of ourselves the part that just wants to love and be loved, we reassure the child within us. Each of us can become entirely that loved child, full of confidence and clear knowing that all is well. In that safe space, the inner child might peek their head out from their blanket fort, maybe even come out to play.

And play it is! The idea of soul mission is not some burden to bear but, rather, a marvelous adventure to undertake, the more consciously the better! And when we invite the Angels along, there is even more fun to be had! Energy seeks equilibrium, so it is natural that the child within us has easier access to Angels than the adult who has been convinced that only what is visible is real.

Darkness Preempting

Again, on the Earth plane, whenever there is a movement toward Light, darkness reacts and responds as an opposing force. This is why when we first start to meditate (stretch toward our Light), darkness/fear responds (fearful thoughts like "Oh, I left the oven on!" or "Darn, I forgot to mail that check!" or "Damn, I forgot my brother's birthday!," designed to get us up from our meditative space). Very effective!

Similarly, when a Lightworker comes on the scene in the form of a child, that new Light attracts darkness—sometimes expressed as difficulties and obstacles, trauma we experience on the path. Nothing is by accident! But even as we recognize the action of darkness in our lives, we must also Re-member that everything happens for a reason, that everything serves, and only a person who has found their way through a jungle can guide others out.

This chapter includes two exercises to tap into that sacred secret part of us that holds the key to Joy: the inner child. First, we will go on a search to find and make that child our partner; then, once teamed up with that part of us most linked to soul and privy to mission, we will begin to do some exercises to find our individual sweet spots, to find our way (back) into (further) alignment.

Ready? Let's go!

Exercise

SEEKING OUT AND TEAMING UP WITH OUR INNER CHILD

As with all energetic protocols discussed in the book, find a spot where you will be undisturbed for a bit. If you have a picture of yourself as a child, you might want to take it out and gaze at it for a bit before you begin. Remember what it was like to be that child, how it felt on a day-to-day basis. Remembering the inner child helps us to Re-member and realign with soul. The child is the closest expression to the form conceived of by soul and Source; the children we were (and still are, deep within) was and is seeded with the blueprint of the Soul mission that is ours.

This exercise will reaffirm the channel opening we did earlier, but this time, we will have the intention to align with the part of us who holds the key to our mission, in Joy, the inner child.

Let's go get 'em!

1 Breathe

Focus on your breath, in and out, and come into a place of peace, at one with the rhythm, expansion and contraction, of the Universe. Remember, breath carries life (and Life): It carried life into your physical body with your first breath and will carry eternal Life out of your body with your last breath. With gratitude toward breath, then, continue focusing on your breath until you feel ready to begin.

2 Set your intention

The most important part of any energy protocol is the intention we bring to it. Set your intention to connect in Love with your inner child, asking

106

for the help of your Angels to do so. Inviting your Guardian Angels along for this work is smart, as they were present when the child you were was walking the earth, so they bore witness to whatever difficulties a sensitive, perspicacious child (you) may have experienced. Also, you might want to invite the lovely mothering energy of the Archangel Gabriel(le) to help fill any lack of tenderness or Love you, as a child, may be carrying related to your experience, such as unloving, harsh treatment from family, friends, teachers, etcetera (even, perhaps, from yourself).

Once your intention is clear . . .

3 Open the channel down to the earth

Building on the channel opening exercise in Chapter 5, use your now-open channel to anchor (ground) yourself, following your beam of Light down to the center of the earth to be bolstered in your task by the consciousness of our Mother Earth. If you wish, repeating a simple phrase from the heart can help here:

Dear Mother, help me to Re-member the child I was, help me to love them and me, as you do, unconditionally. I thank you!

Arriving at the center, notice that Mother Earth/Gaia is waiting for you there, arms wide open. She invites the child within you to leap into her arms—arms that always catch and never disappoint! Once in her loving arms, allow her to fill the child within you with Love and tenderness, unconditionally. Then, when you feel full, with a big "Thank you!" to Gaia, decide to travel up from the heart of the planet to return to your own tender heart. Let yourself be filled with the energy flowing up from Gaia, the Love and tenderness that is true power. Take a moment to absorb all that is there for you, filling you on every level: mental, physical, emotional, spiritual.

When you feel ready . . .

4 Opening the channel up to the heavens

From the level of your heart, beam your light channel up to the heavens, along the spinal cord, through the neck and head, out through the crown chakra, and up to the heavens, a return to Source, where your eternal soul abides. In that space, call on soul (which chose you as a child) to

107

help the reconnection, with words of your own, perhaps something like this . . .

Dear, dear Soul that chose me, thank you for your confidence. I now call on your help in the important work of heart opening, connecting to the child within me who you know so well. Help me to open and understand, Re-member and love. Thank you!

While in the Source space, it is a good time to formally call on our Guardian Angels as well, perhaps something like this:

My dear Guardian Presence, long ago I forgot your Love and neglected to call on your assistance. I permanently shift that now, and with my free will call on your loving aid to find and fill and love and renew the child within me, Love's pure expression. Thank you!

Lastly, while here, you might want to also call on Archangel Gabriel to help you to love the child within (and yourself) unconditionally, communicating more gently and lovingly with yourself:

Archangel Gabriel, help me seek out and love the tender child within me and value their presence, honoring, protecting, and freeing them to express their true nature of Joy and Love in alignment with my soul mission. Thank you!

With each invitation, take a moment and feel or see or know that your prayer is immediately answered. Keep breathing in that Presence, allowing yourself to be filled, and when you are ready, with your Soul and the Angels accompanying you, flow down your beam of light channel into your body, allowing it to be completely filled with celestial light . . .

5 Lighting up your heart—blanket fort of the child

See, feel, or know that when the most tender part of us recoiled and hid from the blustery or dangerous world, the heart space became its blanket fort. Breathe in that celestial Light, and focus it entirely on your heart space. See or feel or know the tender child is there, in front of you, tucked in and hidden under the covers.

Gently, softly, let the child know you are there, that you want to see them, that you came specifically for them.

Stand, feet solid on the ground, shoulder-width apart, shoulders pulled back, with your spinal column straight and tall. This position supports the largest version of your Self possible and is intended to be reassuring and strong. Allow your arms to relax at your sides, palms facing forward in a position of energetic openness. Breathe in the presence of Angels and Archangels all around you. Breathe out anything that blocks your opening to them. Fill your heart with Light and peace, with the Love that is there for you, and that you feel for the child. Take three or four deep breaths at least before continuing.

6 Inviting the child to come out

Imagine the child in front of you stirring under the covers. Invite them to come out, perhaps lifting up a corner of the blanket, allowing the child to be surrounded by Light. Allow the child to emerge at their own pace, until they stand before you, a smaller version of you, at the age that comes up for you naturally.

The child standing there, perhaps wonders which "you" has come this day: the one who forgot about them, the one who is sometimes harsh to them, or the loving adult presence they have been waiting for all this time? You may feel a yearning on the part of the child, or diffidence, or Joy. Whatever it is, accept it, and honor the reaction of this sacred part of your being. The reaction will depend on how you have treated yourself, the most sensitive part of yourself, all these years.

No matter the reaction, if your Intention is clear, then today is the day you will reconnect with the strong Light and Joy, the wide open creativity that is this special child!

There is only one person on the planet who understands fully how difficult things were for this beautiful child, how much they long for safety and Love, and why: you! Remembering the child brings Re-membering. Let the child know that you understand and that you care.

Imagine yourself explaining, perhaps, that you understand how hard it was sometimes, why they started "toughening up," or hiding out. You understand because you were there. You couldn't help then, at the time, because you were small then, too, but now, since you are grown, you can now ensure the safety of the child: bread, safety, and power!

Let the child know how much you value them!

Assure the little one that you will take care of everything if they will only team up with you, that you cannot realize your soul mission without their Joy, their light, their spontaneity restored.

7 With open arms, welcome the child

With everything that needed saying now having been said, it is time to open. Ask the Angels around you to open their wings, creating a perfect holding cocoon of Light and Love around you both, adult and child. Now with Love, open your arms and your heart, inviting the child to trust you, to come into your arms and your heart. Decide that you will be the trust-worthy adult for whom the child has been waiting. Become that uncon-ditionally loving adult, and offer perfect protection (bread, safety, and power). If appropriate, tell them you are sorry for the past, but that the future is wide open in front of you both.

Ask them, "Ready to shine?," and let the child leap into your arms. Be clear that from this day forward, you will always catch them, that you will always catch yourself and hold yourself in Love. Stay in that space, until you feel it is complete.

8 Gratitude—Sealing the deal

Place your hands on your heart to seal the pact between you and the child. See, feel, imagine, or know that the Angels and Archangel Gabriel(le) cover your hands to strengthen the seal, a powerful gesture of solidarity and Unity. Thank the child for trusting you, and thank Archangel Gabriel(le) and your Guardian Angels, as you continue to hold your hands to your chest in a gesture of gratitude for this sacred moment of opening and sounding and Joy and power. Stay in the space until you feel it is complete.

Note: The Aftercare section on page 87 is a good way to help yourself integrate this important work.

Blueprint of the Child

Now that the reconnection has been made, and we have committed to take care of our inner child with loving kindness, the relationship can start us on the path to renewing our purpose and putting in place a program to shift the movement of our lives to return to the natural "sweet spot" flow that will align us with our soul mission.

The underlying premise of the next exercise involves recognizing that there is nothing in us that was not carefully planned by our soul together with Source. Knowing this, we can peel back the layers of everything the world has had us add, those layers we will not need in order to realize our purpose.

Kids come in honest and authentic, unless and until the world screws with us by teaching us that in certain circumstances, our Truth is not appropriate, or in certain situations, our presence or shine is not welcome. Little by little, we adjust to the rules of each situation, and in each adjustment, we lose a bit of that Light the soul placed within us to help us to fully live out our mission. We have seen before that every aspect (strengths and what we consider to be weaknesses) of our being serves that highest purpose. But the world taught us precisely the opposite (which is why we judge ourselves and our attributes to begin with: this is acceptable or valued; that, less so).

The exercise that follows kicks off the more grounded work of harvesting the elements needed, the important values or soul parts, that will be key in creating a plan to shift and Re-member our soul mission and then, to effect it. We remember that the blueprint for this life was sown in us by soul and Source, and so, by uncovering the layers that don't serve, we can find and cultivate the seeds that were planted and consciously bring them to fruition.

You will need a pen and a piece of paper or a notebook for the next exercise, the results of which we will use later on to create a road map to mission!

 Exercise

BLUEPRINT OF THE CHILD

Find a place where you will be calm, a place that is quiet. Have a pen and paper with you, for when the time comes.

1 Open the channel

You know how to do this by now. Let the heart of the earth hold the child that you are, be filled, and then, when you go to the heavens, ask soul and your Angels (Archangel Gabriel and the Guardian Presence) for help, since we will be working with the inner child.

2 Connect with the child

Pick up your child at energetic "daycare," in their blanket fort of the heart. Ask them with Love and tenderness if they want to play with you and the Angels. (They will say yes!)

3 Remember the child

Take a moment or moments to remember what it was like to be the child you were back then. Allow any specific situations that come to mind to play themselves out on the inner screen of your mind (a seat of clairvoyance). Feel the feelings that are there, if any arise. All of this is healing, and all of it inspired by the heavens in grace.

4 Answer the questions

Without thinking, write the first answer that comes to mind for the questions below, no matter how silly it seems, or applicable or not:

- What was your favorite fun thing to do as a child?
- What did you like to eat when you were a child?
- Where did you like to go when you were a kid?
- What was your favorite place in your childhood?
- Who was your favorite adult when you were a child?
- When you were a child, what was there never enough of?
- In your childhood, what was (sadly) missing?
- When you were a child, what did you want more of?
- In your family, what did you never have enough of?
- What do you regret not being able/allowed to do as a child?

Take the time you need to answer each question. For each response, ask yourself, "Why?" until you have a sense of the underlying values that were important to you as a kid (and so, are linked to your soul mission seeding).

Then go back and highlight the underlying values behind the responses that came up for you. These are important because soul seeds the values in us that will most easily (when we don't block ourselves, as seen earlier) lead us to alignment and expression of our soul mission. Be as clear as you can. This work is the foundation of the plan we will set into motion to shift things in the next section.

EXAMPLE: Kathryn's 10 Answers

To give you an idea, here are my answers today. To be clear, I teach this stuff, and every time I teach a workshop, I re-do the exercises. It keeps me "on point" and in my sweet spot. Some elements that were very present in past such exercises (especially safety and security) now show up a bit less, revealing an evolution. It is interesting to re-do the exercise from time to time to get a feel for what is evolving and what our current needs are.

Our answers change not because our experiences of childhood change, but because over time (especially when we are consciously on a spiritual path), we heal certain wounds, and so, they do not jump out at us in the exercise. What comes up for us in the exercise is always what is most germane for our path today.

Kathryn's Questions, Answers, and Underlying Values in Bold

Q: *What was your favorite fun thing to do as a child?*
A: Swim.
Why? I am passionate about **sports,** and I love **water.**

Q: *What was your favorite thing to eat when you were a child?*
A: Fresh fruit.
Why? We didn't have it that often. It was a **natural treat,** and **healthy eating** was rare.

Q: *Where did you like to go when you were a kid?*
A: The swimming pool at Van Cortlandt Park.
Why? Nature and **water** and **sports,** plus I was allowed to go there on my own, so **freedom.**

Q: *What was your favorite place in your childhood?*
A: The library.

Why? Books (lots of 'em!), my **friend** Mary, **candy** (a **treat,** and yes, it was **breaking the rules,** which I found exhilarating . . . lol), and **peace and quiet!**

Q: *Who was your favorite adult when you were a child?*
A: Ms. Conway, my second-grade teacher.
Why? She gave me **attention,** and I felt **safe** with her.

Q: *When you were a child, what was there never enough of?*
A: Peace and quiet.
Why? There was a lot of yelling at home, and a lot of noise outside.

Q: *In your childhood, what was (sadly) missing?*
A: Safety, affection.
Why? Maybe a sign of the times, certainly a cultural thing, and a result of the fact that as seven children, we were more than a handful.

Q: *When you were a child, what did you want more of?*
A: Love and Protection.
Why? Seven children, so not enough love to go around, and traumatic experiences.

Q: *In your family, what did you never have enough of?*
A: Money.
Why? Seven children. The Bronx. You get it.

Q: *What do you regret not being able/allowed to do as a child?*
A: Road Runners Club (they recruited me, but my father said no) and a high school class trip to Paris.
Why? I love **running** and **sports** and so, would have loved to be really **coached** and have **friends** that ran. I also loved **French** and **languages** and dreamed of **travel** in general and going to Paris specifically one day. There was not enough **money,** and there was not enough **freedom** (I was not allowed, very strict upbringing. We can see that this last question might need the most exploring).

Harvesting Gold

Having done the work of remembering the things that were of value to the child you were (whether you actually experienced them, or they were missing), know that none of those values are banal; if they were important to the child you were, they are important to the soul mission.

Spend some time with each element to recognize the importance of each element and why these things emerge from all of your life experiences as a child. Do they speak to you today? Is there an element that pulls you more strongly than others? (As this work was supported and accompanied from on High, what emerged in your answers is no accident, even if there are some things you would rather not remember.)

Take some time to see if you can in some way rank the **values** that emerged in order of their importance to you. Some of the answers to your questions might reveal similar values, such as **attention, affection,** and **love;** put them together in a way that is clear to you, if appropriate. Some answers might reveal more than one underlying value. All of them count, but as you rank them, feel into which values are most important today? Which ones are less important today?

Though the seeding being revealed dates back to your childhood, your evolution since then may have already satisfied certain needs from back then. For example, while I was afraid a lot and needed protection and safety in childhood, I've got it covered now, and it feels like my whole life breaks the traditional "rules," so I have that covered, too. A person who wished for more Love as a child might have created a loving family around them since then. Taking into account our evolution is important, which is why we do the ranking (it will also serve later exercises).

Have fun with it! No pressure! There are no right or wrong answers, only *your* answers! Just notice what you feel most strongly. No one will see this but you, so be honest! Try to get a sense of what is a vital need for you and what is more like a desire or wish.

Here are my ranked values as unearthed in the exercise above, in case that helps:

1 Love and Affection, Friendship
2 Peace and Quiet (rare at home or elsewhere, library)
3 Sports, Exercise
4 Nature, Water

5 Healthy Eating

6 Languages, Travel

7 Books (reading and writing)

8 Mentor (teacher, coach)

9 Money

10 Freedom

11 Safety/Protection

12 Breaking the Rules

Notice what emerges as you do the ranking. The list comes from childhood, but the ranking is where you stand now!

In this crazy world, we do not always take time to see how we have grown. For example, I notice I now place the values of Safety/Protection and Rule Breaking at the bottom of my list. This is not because they are no longer important (they are!), but because these are needs I have already worked out and consciously satisfy, values I have already tangibly expressed for myself in my life as it is today.

The desires and needs that come out of this exercise are important to address in order to live out our soul mission, either because, like books being on my list, they represent a part of our soul mission, or because they represent a blockage to living in our sweet spot, aligning with soul and our mission. When we satisfy the needs from childhood, we dissolve blockages on our path like those we explored in Chapter 6.

All elements that came up as important from childhood were seeded in us to support our soul mission, so hang onto the list. We will be adding other values that are very important to our soul mission in the next chapter of Re-membering.

Chapter 8

RE-MEMBERING FURTHER—
SECRET DREAM, INNER GPS,
FRIENDS, AND IDOLS

*T*he exercise we did in the previous chapter reveals what values and desires were planted in us at the beginning of our life path by soul and Source, even before we were born. In the boat analogy, we can imagine them as being like rudders or our unique inner GPS system, that we can steer our life by.

To confirm this, just look at any siblings or cousins who may have grown up in your immediate or extended family. Do you all have the same interests? Probably not! Now, think of your parents, if you have a memory of them. Do you have all the same interests? Again, probably not—not entirely, anyway!

This shows us that we are unique beings with personal desires that are not shared by everyone. The desires and capacities that are unique to us are always connected to why we came into the world on a soul level, as our soul with Source chose and designed us perfectly for the mission.

This is why we began our digging for gold with the experience of the inner child, the child we were, since the child has fewer layers covering the soul's plantings.

Sometimes, though, our path calls to us midstream on our path; that is, as adults. A "chance" encounter (there is no such thing!) with people, places, or things can divert the Flow of our lives and cause us to change direction, like the woman with the amethyst who catalyzed my leaving a bar stool for the Life that awaited me.

Such encounters are always **soul contracts** (in the case of people) or **soul markers** (in the case of things or places). Let's take a look at these, so they will be more recognizable.

Soul Contracts and Our Mission

People on Our Path

We have already mentioned that soul contracts are experiences with other people that mark us, and that create a context for growth and aligning with our mission. While on the terrain, we may judge these experiences as "positive" or "negative," but on an eternal, soul mission scale, they are at worst "neutral" (imagine if I had lost the amethyst or paid no heed) and at best (very) "helpful."

Example of soul contracts through experiences we deem "positive" might be expressed as a favorite teacher, such as my Miss Conway in the Q&A in Chapter 7; a mentor in our lives who guides us, perhaps into a different career; or that "special someone" we end up marrying. The soul contract tradeoff is perhaps most clear in these "positive" scenarios: each person is supported on their journey by the presence of the other.

"Negative" experiences can be more difficult to recognize as beneficial, but there is always something important that opens a door when a soul contract expresses in this way, though our humanity howls at the idea (not seeing such contexts from the Higher, eternal, perspective). Such "negative" soul contracts can express themselves as mistreatment, abuse, even violence. While part of us may be loathe to lend credence to the idea that these are in any way "good," it may be helpful to remember that "There is no place that God is not." Who We Are, Truly is always safe in the loving arms of God. Our soul never disidentified with Source; it is us who forgot (for the purposes of the game of Life). So as real as these experiences seem, we are living them on a stage, as players, while the Truth of who we are is safe underneath our makeup and human costume.

"What good can come out of abuse or violence?" you may ask. I agree. It is not an easy nut to chew. But imagine that there is mistreatment in a marriage. This may give the suffering person the courage to leave, to affirm themselves, in alignment with their soul purpose. For the persecutor, balancing karma or seeking redemption might be on the table.

In the case of child abuse, no matter the degree, it can leave one distrustful. But when we grow through it (if indeed, we use our free will to seek help and work through it), we can emerge more powerful and more compassionate, and in an excellent place to help others who went through similar issues. As for the perpetrator: In this case, the soul that is the aggressor agreed to take on the role that would bring them hatred and self-loathing (in the name of karmic balancing and redemption, perhaps). Every soul is on its own path.

Note: This is not to condone such actions, but rather, to give another perspective, an eternal one, that is not caught up in the drama playing out on Earth but focused on the truth of Who We Are, Truly and why we are here.

Soul contract experiences, positive or negative as they may be viewed, can lead us to live or work in different places, leading us to new experiences, which then align us further with our soul mission. As noted earlier, new places and things on our path that invite a shift in alignment are called "soul markers" and also guide us to our soul mission. We will look at them shortly.

Family Soul Contracts—Having Children

Some of the most important soul contracts we may have are with spouses and children, if we have them. These souls have emerged from Source to play the Game at our side, at least for part of our time here on Earth. As life partner or parent, our impact on these souls is very likely part of our mission.

Our children are not ours by accident. These days, with the world straddling what was and what will be, our early experience may be rooted in what was, but the souls that are emerging into the Game as our children are preparing for, or already aligned with, what will be: a world that is not here yet, founded on Love and freedom, not obligation and fear.

If you feel that this applies to you and your children, it is very likely an important part of your mission to be a parent to these children, and in so doing, create a bridge from the old to the new. If you and your life partner are not particularly energetically aligned on this matter, perhaps the two of you represent the old and the new, thus giving the children a taste of both, so there is more ease in the transition.

If being a parent is on your life path; that is to say, if you are a parent (because parenting is always a soul choice, even in situations where it seems to be more a surprise than a choice), relax and be yourself. Their soul (along with God) chose you as parent because your way of being is exactly what the child will need to grow toward (or rebel from) to serve out their mission. Often when parents come to see me, saying their children are having a hard time finding their way in a world that is not (yet) suited to them, where the old molds are broken or don't fit, and the new do not yet exist, the message from the Angels is this: Stay true to yourself, and shine your Light. This will be the ideal example for the souls that have come to you as children. This is always a soul contract, and your alignment will support theirs.

Soul Markers—Places and Things on Your Path

At times, the soul contracts in our lives lead us to soul markers; at other times, the reverse is true. No matter. The people, places, and things that will help us Re-member will come up along our path, and if we miss them, they will come up again, perhaps in a different form.

Soul Marker Things Are Signs

Like a lucky charm or a talisman, a rosary, or a holy book, or a guitar or dance shoes, soul markers are things that help us align with our soul and mission.

It may be that the first time we saw a guitar we just had to play it. A shark tooth that came to us on the surf or a shell we found on the beach on a special day can take on a special meaning for us. A wedding ring, a credit card, a lucky scarf—different things that take on a special importance to us along the way, that carry an energy that feels supportive to us, are soul markers. I have a few of these, like the amethyst crystal I got at the bank, and each one keeps me in alignment in its own way.

It is important to note that it is not only objects that in themselves become important on our journey but also the objects that draw our attention to something or someone that will be important on our path. For example, imagine someone is wearing a very bright hat, which catches our attention, drawing our eyes to the person standing next to them. And then, we can't take our eyes off them.

The Shark Tooth in the following story is one of my favorite soul markers on my journey.

Shark Tooth

I was walking along the water in Emerald Isle, North Carolina, in the off-season, so there was no one there but me and the pelicans and dolphins. I had had an intense meditation session that morning and was in the process of writing *Inviting Angels into Your Life,* so I had done just that: I invited the Angels to walk with me.

Along the way, I remembered an odd encounter I had had on this beach a few days prior, where a man had alerted me to the fact that there were many shark teeth on the beach (logical, since there are many sharks in the waters), so it occurred to me (thank you Angels!) to start to look for some.

As most of them are small and blackened, it is easy to mistake a broken black shell piece for a shark's tooth; only touching them can confirm or refute the truth of it. I walked along, and picked up this and that, chuckling to myself each time I was wrong, and finally asked the Angels to assist.

A few minutes later, I saw in the shallow water something that had the distinctive triangular form and black color that so often denoted a shark tooth. When I got to it, I bent over to pick it up, but even as I lowered my sights (literally), I saw that it was a broken shell. But then, oh, the most amazing thing happened! Before I could stand up again, a small wave came in, carrying on it . . . a shark tooth! And not just any shark tooth! This one was not black, but whitish-gray and brown, and it was much larger than what I had been looking for, almost the size of my pinky!

Out of 24 miles of beach, at that moment when I had asked the Angels for help with my search, a unique and large shark tooth came floating right up to me on a wave directly to where I was crouching to look.

In this, we can see that an object, a thing, can play a role in the Universe encouraging us and communicating with us in order to help us stay aligned with our mission. A soul marker!

Remember: The idea is not to make an idol out of a thing, but to remember that there is no place that God is not, and everything, but also "every thing" happens for a reason. When we realize this, we begin to keep our eyes open for such soul markers, which will either be recognizable in the moment, through physical reaction (like me crying when the shark tooth arrived, or chills when we see a sign from a loved one who has passed), or we will see their significance after the fact.

Soul Marker Places

A soul marker might be a thing or a place. When we arrive at a soul marker place, our human experience might be "positive" or "negative," but we recognize it as making a mark on our journey. In fact, whether we deem the experience "positive" or "negative" is often a function of whether we see the place in the grand scheme of our soul mission or not.

An extreme negative experience of place might be going to prison, but prison is just the sort of "time out" place that might bring a person to consciousness. Another negative might be a school we hated, or a place we lived where we weren't happy, all of which will impact and refine our choices afterward.

Positive experiences of place can be extreme (my attraction to Paris, for example, when there were no French influences in my Bronx childhood). In this case, it might be a place we dream of visiting, and when we arrive, the dream seems somehow to be activated, and sometimes our body will react with tears or goosebumps or energy flowing through us in waves. Each person's instrument plays differently. How does your instrument let you know when you are in a special place?

EXAMPLE: Attitude Adjustment Cottage
(Emerald Isle, North Carolina)

When I was still a banker, a new expatriate living in Paris, I got a windfall bonus that I decided to use as a down payment on a house on the beach, a childhood dream of mine.

I took to the internet and searched up and down the East Coast of the United States, looking for the cheapest house on the beach I could find. The result was Attitude Adjustment, the name of the cottage on the beach on the southern Outer Banks of North Carolina, in Emerald Isle, where I was when the shark tooth came up to me. There were many barriers to purchase—the foundation pylons needed to be redone, and the zoning regulations in this hurricane-prone place were daunting; however, this made my choice less expensive and, therefore, possible, so I found the realtor and went forward with the purchase.

The day of signing was set for my first day off during a business trip back to bank headquarters in Charlotte, North Carolina. I flew out to the coast and rented a car to head to the island, first calling the realtor to let him know I wanted to actually physically visit the house before I signed the deal. He understood, of course, so an hour or so later, we mounted the steps to the front door together, and he opened the door for me. We stepped in, and oh, I was home! I knew it, felt it to my bones, and started crying.

After reassuring the realtor that these were good tears, we went and signed the papers. The house rents out most of the year, a wonderful place for people seeking sea and sand, sky and surf. But every year or so, I go in the off-season and write or teach—or catch wind of the Angels through shark teeth.

Places that feed our soul are evident: we feel good when we are there. We know such places by a strange sense of familiarity in a new place, and our bodies will often confirm our knowing by reacting (tears, goosebumps, heat, etcetera).

Question

In aligning with soul mission, it is good to ask ourselves, what are the places, or types of places, that feed our soul?

The answer to this question belongs on our lists of values. Mine is a value that is already on that list: **Nature/Water.** If your answer is not on your list of underlying values, add it now.

Other Exercises to Find Underlying Values for Soul Mission

We have touched on the so-important inner child work to gather information for our soul mission alignment, our Re-membering, and soul markers along the way in the forms of people, places, and things, but let's take a look at some other elements and do exercises that will round out our list of values aligned with our mission: Secret Dream, Who Are Your Friends?, and Who Do You Admire/Who Does What You Wish You Could Do?

Secret Dream

We have already seen that our dreams were seeded in us by soul and Source before we were born, and after we were born, our experiences as children and whether Love was abundant or not either rendered us confident or less so. All of this impacts our dreams, and whether we live them, share them, or keep them a secret!

When we are confident in life and encouraged, we may dare to pursue the dreams that fill our heart. But what about when we are not confident, when our life experience has *not* encouraged us? What about the dreams we don't dare to go after? Or the dreams of which we don't even dare speak?

 Exercise

SECRET DREAM

1 **Close your eyes,** and find that internal space you have been cultivating here. Invite your Angels to help.
2 **Imagine** a friend in front of you, someone you could consider a "cheerleader" for your Life Game.
3 **Imagine** that your cheerleader asks you this question: What has been your secret dream?
4 **Notice** what comes up, maybe a few things; some paths that you would have liked to have followed. Of these, which is the one you *don't* want to share, the one you don't even want to say aloud for fear that it would sound too ridiculous, even in "safe" company? That is your secret dream!

Our secret dream is one that (maybe since forever) you wish you had pursued, or could pursue, yet you keep it secret. If your dream is something you can't or don't talk about, if it is a secret dream, we should pay even more attention! Why is that?

Why wouldn't we talk about having a dream, not even in general terms? The answer is fear—fear is always what blocks us! For the most part, we don't share our secret dreams when we are afraid people will mock us for them. And with our most important dreams, that would be insufferable! Imagine having a dream as like having a baby. How would we feel if we had a baby we love so much and people made fun of them?

So fear is blocking our sharing and realization of the secret dream, but our soul mission is all about the opposite, Love. Makes sense, right? When we stretch toward our Light (Love), darkness reacts to dissuade us (fear).

Here's the thing, though: The bigger the Love (the soul's movement behind an action), the more fear we will have around sharing it. Unconsciously, we can be frightened by our own Light, and so without knowing why, unable to pursue it. This truth hides some very good news, however: *The more fear there is around our dream, the sweeter our spot will be; that is, the more Love will spread by the living of it.*

For this reason, our secret dream, if we have one, is a very potent ally in our search to Re-member our soul mission. Sharing our dreams with others is very personal and intimate; it makes us vulnerable, and thus, can evoke fear (we will speak later about finding the right people with whom to share our dreams, our cheerleaders). But if we have a secret dream, one we don't share, we can be very sure that it is high up there on the soul mission list, so add it to your underlying values list!

EXAMPLE: Keeping Dreams a Secret

When I was a banker, and not very happy, I almost never spoke to anyone about my desire for a more spiritual life. Once, when I did speak that Truth to one person (my first "love"), he laughed at me, and even joked with his friends about it.

Oh, I learned my lesson, alright! From that experience, back then, I took the lesson to keep the important stuff to myself. I also

wondered if maybe he wasn't right—maybe it was a bit ridiculous after all; maybe it was time to grow up.

Of course, my takeaways were both right . . . and wrong. The
discernment I learned from that situation is still a golden rule for
me today: I was guilty of giving away my "baby" to someone
who wouldn't, or couldn't, care for it. Now I know better (discernment), but the underlying values, the secret yearning of the heart,
will always be called ridiculous by those who don't understand.

Later, much later, I also learned that it is never too late, not
if the soul is still yearning for something. It is when the yearning
is over (when we have killed it, perhaps) that the mission and
thus, Life with a capital L is lost.

So what is your secret dream? Why? Figure out the value, the soul seeding,
within your dream, then add it to your list, as we did in the Inner Child
exercise, because such values are profoundly important.

For me today, as much as I do not want to talk about this, mine is
singing. I have always sung and loved to do that as a child but wasn't
allowed to sing at home. So I guess I will add it to my list. (**Note:** Adding
something like "singing" to our list does not necessarily mean we are meant
to be professional singers, but that our soul longs for us to sing!)

Who Are Your Friends?

Throughout our journey together, we have taken note of a few great Truths,
such as, "There is no place that God is not," and the Universal Laws of
Energy, including, "Where our attention goes, so goes our energy that
creates" and the famous "Energy seeks equilibrium."

It is on that last one that our next exercise relies. "Energy seeks equilibrium" basically reminds us of what we already know: "Apples don't fall far
from the tree," "Money finds money," "Takes one to know one," etcetera.

The way this works, as we saw earlier, is that we have an energetic field
around us, and we have filled that field with our thoughts, words, emotions,
dreams, and desires. What is in our field attracts others who have similar
things in their field, even when we didn't even know that the elements were
important to us!

So here is the question that continues us along the path toward soul
mission, gleaning still other (or reinforcing the same) values:

Who are your friends? Who are the people around you?

What are their interests, passions, and dreams?

If you see some resonance in the people around you, in what they do and what they value, it is likely that those values are high on the soul list for you, too! This is why many "secret dream" actors become agents, many "secret dream" writers become editors, and why music lovers are attracted to music makers!

Once you have an answer, understand that the activities are values that are energetically attracting you to these people. Something in their energetic field is calling to something in your field. What is it? How can this Truth contribute to your soul mission?

Kathryn's Answers—
Musicians, Writers, People on a Spiritual Path

As ever, I share my own answers with you here to accompany your work:

- **Musicians:** I am nourished by music. I was not allowed to learn **guitar** as a child, and I still want to do this. Also singing. Also listening to music more and allowing **time** for this.
- **Writers/Poets Especially:** Even as a child, I have always written, especially poetry. But I secret-dreamed poetry long ago—time to take it out from under the blanket fort!
- **Spiritual Path:** Yes, indeed. This is already a priority, so it is natural that I attract people who have already stepped onto their spiritual path, and people who are getting ready to do so. (Of course, stepping onto our spiritual path is simply recognizing that our path, every element of it, is already spiritual!)

Whatever you have gleaned from this exercise, if it is not already on your list of values from page 112, add it. (I will be adding poetry and guitar and taking the time for music.)

Who Do You Admire? Who Does What You Wish You Could Do?

This last exercise, which will complete the list of values that are important to our soul mission (either because they represent the expression of our purpose or a blockage to it that needs to be healed) is linked to both energy seeking equilibrium and where our attention goes, so goes our energy.

In this exercise, we will look at what values and gold nuggets of treasure we might find when we take an honest look at who we most admire, and maybe also, of whom we might be jealous.

Jealousy has two definitions: it is both the coveting of something that someone else has and the close vigilance with which they might guard it or we might guard the secret of it. We can see the difference in this sentence: "I jealously guarded the secret that I was jealous of them."

In fact, most of us would jealously guard such a secret! After all, jealousy is one of the infamous Seven Deadly Sins (Catholic school, much?); definitely not something of which we might be proud! For that reason, if you do not want to work with jealousy, you can do the exercise below with the idea of very strong admiration, if you like, but envy or jealousy is a more direct route, when possible. Call it "People I Admire Greatly Who Do Something I Wish that I Could Do," for example.

But what if I told you that jealousy (unless acted upon) is not negative but neutral; simply a source of information, and in our case, information vital to our soul mission?

Huh?

Imagine that our body is our vehicle (it is), and "jealousy" as simply one of the instrument displays on the dashboard, like a gas gauge. When we are jealous, our gauge "lights up"; that is, we become very attentive, very vigilant toward a person of whom we are jealous. Unfortunately, people who don't fully understand what the instrument panels mean (or how to drive their vehicle), crash; they make it personal, when it is, in fact, not at all personal!

When we look at jealousy in this neutral, informational way, it strongly attracts our attention to what we truly want on a soul level. Like a gas gauge that tells us that it is time to "fill 'er up!," jealousy that might be aroused in us can give us good guidance with regard to which road to take from where we are today, where our soul wants us to go!

Now, I am not talking about small envies, such as of a watch or a car, but rather jealousy of a career, relationship, or any success, however that expresses. (For this reason, we can indeed use the term "admiration," instead of jealousy, if it makes us more comfortable.)

Our physical instrument, the body, is full of wisdom. It reacts, and that is often how we come to know when we might be feeling jealous or envious of someone else. In this, our vehicles can drive us to our next destination!

 **Exercise**

WHO DO YOU ADMIRE, AND WHO DOES WHAT YOU WISH YOU COULD DO?

1 Breathe in and out, and become quiet. Have a pen and paper ready.
2 Set the intention to open up and receive the information most important to you on your path to soul mission.
3 Open the channel, asking Mother Earth to allow your body to express clearly what you need to know, and ask your Angels to accompany you.

Note: Inviting your Guardian Angels in is a great idea, because they know what the original plan is, and they probably had a hand in both setting it and in making sure that people have crossed your path or come to your attention who are already experiencing and manifesting elements of your soul path. Inviting Archangel Michael to support you is highly recommended, as He helps Lightworkers to find their way. Also He can help us to avoid the trap of judging ourselves harshly (as the world, which understands does not see the clarity value of jealousy). Judging ourselves is judging our vehicle, and it makes no sense, just as it would make no sense to blame our gas gauge if we were to run out of gas. As this is a clear step towards our Light and power, it is well to invite the Power of God, Michael, along for support.

4 Close your eyes, and ask the Angels to show you who you are meant to work with: either who you most admire (people who do things you would love to do also) or who does what you wish you could do (who is already living out your secret desire, perhaps? Who is living the life you wanted, if only?). These can be people you know, family or friends, co-workers, or people you don't know. They can be famous people who are alive, or famous people who have died. In a pinch, they can also be Saints or Ascended Masters you admire greatly, but it may be better to begin for the first time with people who are more accessible.

5 When you have a clear sense of who it will be good for you to work with, write their names down on a page. (Try to keep this to a maximum of three people.)

6 For each person, write why you admire them greatly/or wish you could do what they do. Be as specific as you can. If it is a writer, maybe what type of writing makes you admire them? Is it form or style, or something else? For each person, note at least one thing you esteem about them, and if applicable, be as specific as possible with regard to what it is about them that creates a jealousy light on the dashboard of your vehicle.

7 Thank your Angels, Archangel Michael, and all of the beings who came up on your list.

When you have finished, look at your answers and identify the values that are expressed by your three people. Note what echoes from the work already done, and note anything new. We will use the information in the next section.

Kathryn's Answers Today

To give you an idea of how this might look, here are my answers today: three people, and what I greatly admire about them that I wish I could do:

1 John Denver—He played guitar and wrote/sang songs of spiritual power.

2 Mary Oliver—Her poetry is nature-based and spiritually powerful.

3 Jodie Foster—This American of about my age speaks French flawlessly, with no accent.

I note that *guitar, singing,* and *spiritual power,* as well as *nature* and *poetry* echo elements already found in the earlier exercises. *Actress* and *French without an accent* are new values, so I add them to my list.

EXAMPLE: Why This Exercise Is Important

This exercise can lead us to going places, but not always where we think we are headed!

Years ago, when I was abruptly (if happily) no longer a banker, I did a similar exercise, which pointed me to Jodie Foster, but with an altogether different specificity. I was jealous of her acting. When I was a child, I asked my parents to take me to an open casting call for Annie, a play that was going to be on Broadway. They laughed; ergo, "secret dream"!

So, after 22 years of working in a job I did not love, I focused on Jodie Foster. The uncovering of this desire in me surprised and delighted me. Imagining that I was going to be the next Jodie Foster (or better, the next Kathryn Hudson), and I set off to acting school right after my job closed out.

But on a spiritual path, often we are only given next steps and not the whole vista. Little did I know that years of shutting all my doors had to be undone for me to act, because that art requires the actor to be fearless in expressing and revealing their emotions to others. Only true emotion can touch hearts, so I learned (first at Acting International in Paris, and then at Pygmalion Studio) how to undo all that hiding and shutting down. I also eventually Re-membered how to relax and have fun again.

The work I did there was not a precursor to an acting career, but to my work as a spiritual teacher and guide, for which authenticity and the audacity of vulnerability is also required.

So, as you do the exercises herein, remember that you may think you know where it will lead, but the Angels work on a need-to-know basis! From my perspective, I can say that they are right. If I had known what was ahead of me on the path—that I would become a spiritual teacher—I would have run for cover, screaming, in the opposite direction, maybe straight to the pub.

You now have a list of underlying values, wonderful nuggets of gold, and building blocks for your soul plan. Ready? Let's go!

Part Three

ALIGNING WITH YOUR SOUL MISSION WITH HELP FROM THE ANGELS

Chapter 9

THE PORTAL

When our soul and our Angels nudge us to pull the covers back on our blanket fort strongly enough, we might well begin to take the Game, our Life and our mission, more seriously, asking the big questions: "Why am I here?," "Am I happy?," and "What do I value?"

Angels do it through miracles, defined here as "When God/Angels touch humanity." They can happen though interventions like the woman who came into the bank with the amethyst to give me that powerful nudge.

Angelic nudging often comes from outside of us: They try to attract our attention, wake us up, with signs that can range from feathers or sharks teeth or Guardian Angel "saves" in near-death experience scenarios. Angelic interventions are powerful tools, but they usually come into play when the subtler efforts of their partner, our soul, have been tried without success.

In contrast to the Angels' way, our soul prods and urges us from within our very being, which is also the soul's being, of course: the Truth being that we are One. Subtly, within, when it is time for us to grow into alignment with our soul and mission, we might begin to feel restless, a growing sense of dissatisfaction with how our life is, with any or all of its major elements: work, relationship, health, etcetera. It may be that we weren't really satisfied before, either, but when soul comes calling, what we could put up with before is no longer possible. We are pushed into growing, whether or not we like it, and perhaps we can imagine the comforting scene of our soul (with our Angels and God) leaning over us whispering, "Grow, grow!"

When it's time, it's time! No sense in beating ourselves up over any time wasted. There are no coincidences, and any time we deem "wasted" blocks our understanding of how that time actually served us. If having followed all the rules for a life the world deems a success lands us with an empty feeling, wondering if after all we had not settled, it might just be time to take a look within, to see if we need to get off the worldly "success express" (playing life by the world's rules), and look instead into derailing that express in order to get on board with our soul!

It is never too late! We already have an understanding of how "the game" works: who we are on a soul level, why we are chosen on a human level, who is there to help us as allies. We have looked theoretically at The Forgetting of Who We Are Truly, our soul and mission, and The Re-membering, and lived through that Forgetting and probably at least part of the Re-membering, as you are reading this in real life.

We opened wide our channels to access both the strengths of our human aspect through our Mother Earth. We have looked closely at the blockages to our Re-membering of soul and mission, and gathered the gold, piece by piece, of the values that are innate within us, planted there to be discovered by our soul, like Easter eggs.

Most importantly, perhaps, we have seen that the experience we had as a child is a key to unlocking that door, since the child we were (who still exists within us) was, and is, more connected to our soul than the adult version of us could ever be.

Now, let us go through that door together: child, adult, soul, in the company of Angels.

Going through the Portal

We begin by imagining a conversation between your soul and, well, you!

It begins with the soul saying something like the following:

"If you are in agreement, today is the day!"

Huh?

"Well, nothing happens without your accord (that whole free will thing), so today is the day only if you agree! Got it?"

What day?

"You know, *the* day—the day the whole Universe has been waiting for! (You are perfectly on time, though, no worries!)

Wait! What? What day??

"Only the day where you shift gears on your vehicle . . ."

What does that mean?

"Well, we can agree, can't we, that The Forgetting was pretty powerful, and you lost sight of how powerful you are? And that the noise of the world along with its shiny, shiny things distracted you from your mission by its sights and sounds?"

Well, I don't know . . .

"Okay, well, can we agree that you feel like something is missing?"

That? Yes, definitely!

"Great. And that you would like to do something about that?"

That, too, yes, definitely!

"Now we're getting somewhere! So do you agree that today is the day that we start doing something about it?"

Ah, yes, of course. That's what I'm here for!

Yes, that is what you are here for, and what I am here for, and what this book is about, and why we are "meeting" here, like this, at this moment.

Today is the day, now is the moment, the only moment, that there ever is, the only moment that is possible.

Today, a "vehicle shift" is planned. In the past, your path advanced in reactivity, unconscious of the soul and mission, spontaneously, and in line with what the world put forth as the possibilities. Now, the invitation is extended to align consciously with your unique soul and mission, and never to let the prize out of your sight again!

Imagine we had an automobile, but then we switched to a car that drove itself exactly where we needed to go for the most Joy possible!

This is not a case of ceding our power to an outside force (because the soul is us, the eternal aspect of us), but rather humbly allowing God to take the driver seat and sitting back and enjoying the ride! Sound good?

Remembering always that our free will means we can get off the ride whenever we wish, today is still a big day, as it represents new doors opening for our vehicle. In continuing, we invoke a space for grace, a co-creation with the Divine aspect of ourselves, our soul, with the Angels, with God.

If that sounds good, then you have a clear intention. We already know that our intentions create. In addition, your clear intention is "inspired"; that is, it is a gift of Re-membering from the heavens, a nudging of your soul, with a little help from your Friends in High Places, the Angels.

To reinforce the intention and get the creating started, we just need a ritual. I have just the thing! Let's get started, with an exercise I call The Portal.

Exercise
THE PORTAL

The preliminaries of this exercise are the same as in previous work we have done together. We will be opening and activating our instrument, the body, with breath, followed by setting intention and opening the channel.

You can do this in the way I propose here or in some other way. If you choose to do it another way, go directly to step 5, where we connect again with our inner child. It will be important to do this work again, to solidify this important connection.

Let's begin!

1 Breathe

Focus on your breath, in and out, to come into a place of peace, at one with the rhythm, expansion and contraction, of the Universe. Remember, breath carries life and Life. It carried physical life into our body with our first breath and will carry eternal Life out of the body with our last. With gratitude, then, toward breath and your breathing, continue until you feel ready.

2 Set your intention

The most important part of any energetic protocol is the intention we bring to it. Set your intention to pass through the portal of unconscious life to conscious Life, aligned with soul and mission, asking the help of your Angels to do so.

Inviting our Guardian Angels is a good idea, as they were there when your soul struck a deal to enter the game of Life on Earth with a very precise intention, and they were also there when soul and Source chose to entrust the mission to you.

You may want to also invite the powerful energy of Archangel Michael, with His machete/sword to cut through the jungle and create a clear pathway.

Take a moment to allow that Presence, and your strong intention to settle. Then . . .

3 Open the channel down to the earth

Building on the channel-opening exercises we have already done, use your now open channel to anchor (ground) yourself, beaming your light down to the center of the earth, to be bolstered in your task of realizing your soul mission by the consciousness of our Mother, Earth. If you wish, a simple phrase from the heart can help here:

Dear Mother, help me to Re-member the mission I was born to serve, help me to Love, and to create as you do, powerfully. Thank you!

Arriving at the center, Gaia/Mother Earth is as ever waiting for you, arms open wide. She enfolds you, bringing you into her chest, while her hand presses gently against your third eye.

Allow her to fill you with Love and tenderness and clarity of mission and purpose. Since she knows your soul mission will also help her transformation, feel the gratitude and respect flowing from her heart to yours, and the sense of oneness of purpose and being that is there. Take all you need, all the talents and strengths you will need to joyfully follow on with your journey to success in your mission.

When you feel full, with a big "Thank you!" to Gaia, travel up from the heart of the planet and return to your own clear heart. Let yourself be filled with the energy flowing up from Gaia, clarity, Love, and gentle power. Take a moment to absorb all that is there for you, "filling up" on every level: mental, physical, emotional, spiritual, then, grounded and ready . . .

4 Open the channel up to the heavens

From the level of your heart, beam your Light channel up to the heavens, along the spinal cord, through the neck and head, out through the crown chakra, and up to the heavens, a return to Source, where your eternal soul abides. In that space, call on soul to help your Re-membering, with words of your own, perhaps something like:

Dear, shining soul of Source that chose me, thank you for your trust. I call on you now to help me in the important work before us, aligning my human life purpose to your sacred mission. Of my own free will, I do this today; this day and all the days that follow, stay close to me and to the child within me that you know so well. Help me to open and understand, Re-member and Love. Thank you!

While in the Source space, it is a good time to formally call on our Guardian Angels as well. This is best expressed in your own words from the heart, but could be something like:

I call on the Guardian Presence of God around me, my Guardian Angels, which know me better than even I know myself. Long ago, I forgot your Love and neglected to call on your assistance. I shift that now, and with my free will call on your loving aid to guide, protect, and accompany me this day across the threshold of darkness to Light, of confusion to clarity, and of fear to Love. Carry me forward this day, and all days to come, in ever clearer ways. Thank you!

Lastly, while here, it is a good time to formalize our call to Archangel Michael to step up with us into our power. This, too, is always best expressed in your own words, but could sound something like:

I call on the Presence of the Power of God, Archangel Michael, who knows my Lightworker role better than I know it myself, to guide, protect, and accompany me as I step consciously and powerfully into the role for which I was born. Carry me forward this day, and all days to come, in ever clearer ways. Thank you!

With each invitation, take a moment and feel or see or know that your prayer is immediately and powerfully answered. Keep breathing in that Light and Power of Presence. Allow yourself to be filled, and when you are ready, with your soul and the Angels accompanying you, Flow down your beam of Light channel into your body, allowing it to be completely filled with celestial Light . . .

5 Lighting up your heart—Blanket fort of the child

Knowing that when the most tender part of us recoiled and hid from the blustery or dangerous world, the heart space itself became its blanket fort. Breathing in celestial Light, focus it entirely on your heart space. See or feel or know that the tender child is there, the one with the key to the Portal, to the mission, to the Joy, tucked in and hidden under the covers.

Gently, softly, let the child know you are there, that you want to see them, that you came specifically for them, for their help on a great adventure. Breathing in ever more Light, fill your invitation with its Love.

6 Inviting the child to leave the blanket fort—The journey out

See or feel or know the child before you stirring under the blanket fort. Invite them to come out, perhaps by lifting up a corner of the blanket so that the child is surrounded by Light. Allow the child to emerge at their own pace, until they stand in front of you, a smaller version of you, at the age that comes up for you naturally. If your intention is clear, and today is the day, extend your hand to the child, inviting them to walk with you on the path of life. Let them know that they hold the key to this door, a Portal to strong Light and Joy, and the wide-open creativity that is within them!

Shyly, perhaps, at first, then with more confidence at each step, let the child come along at their own pace until at some point it may seem even as if they are leading you!

Let the child know how much you value them!

Thank them for having left the comfort of their blanket fort. Offer them reassurance that you will ensure their safety but that you are not alone in this: soul, the Angels, and Archangel Michael and his sword are with you both, protecting you, supporting the mission, and rendering the crooked path straight.

Relax and enjoy the scenery, as you follow a lovely path through a forest, passing under boughs and scrambling over rocks together, finally together! As you pass a small but very high waterfall, you slow to hear what sounds like laughter, as the water sprites and elementals, other children of Gaia all around you, celebrate this day with you!

Notice that the path is mounting now, winding a bit but still easy, so you are not even out of breath when you reach the high tree line where all is clear. You arrive together, adult and child, the two of you ready, excited, to meet up with soul, to go forward Re-membered, to go forward with the Angels to secure the mission.

Just then, you arrive at a sort of plateau, as if the top of the mountain had been chopped off by an exquisite sculptor. And there, in the center of the flat shining space, you see it . . .

7 The Portal!

It is as you knew it would be. Each person's Portal is unique, and the doorway can take many forms. How does it come to you? You may see it in your mind's eye, or you may imagine it as the child in you wishes it to be. No matter! (Mine is in mother-of-pearl and opens and closes slowly, like an abalone.)

Turn to your child, and ask, "Ready to shine?," and let the child lead you to the doorway, in the company of your Angels. If the door you see is closed, open it yourself, or ask the child or your Angels to do it. Then the most important part: stepping through!

When you step through this Portal, you are agreeing to align your human life purpose with your soul's mission. In your free will, you are choosing that this be so, and that the child within you is freed in this way to joyfully create next steps.

8 Stepping through

Approach the threshold, and see or imagine, feel or know, that your soul is waiting, smiling, just on the other side. When the time is right, step (or leap), hand in hand with your inner child, straight into the arms of your soul.

Give yourself time to see what is on the other side of the door, if there is a terrain, a path, or perhaps simply (and magnificently) brilliant Light. Feel how nice it is to be with your soul in this way, feel or know your expansion like a homecoming, the Re-membering we have been waiting for since the beginning. Stay in that space until you feel complete.

9 Gratitude seals the deal

Place your hands on your heart to seal the pact between you (adult and child) and your soul. Know that the Angels and Archangel Michael cover your hands to strengthen the seal, in a powerful gesture of solidarity and Unity. Thank your soul for entrusting its mission to you, holding your hands to your chest in a continuing gesture of gratitude for this sacred moment of opening and sounding and Joy and Power. Stay in the space until you feel complete.

Note: The Aftercare section on page 87 is a good way to help yourself integrate this important work.

Once you have completed the exercise, notice specifically if anything new came out of the experience in terms of values. What did you see on the other side of the portal? Any clues to what comes next?

For me, the terrain is always rolling hills and abundant **Nature,** confirming the value I already have on my list of values, and the raw material we will use in the coming chapters, as we work on aligning our human plan with our soul plan for the mission.

Chapter 10

MANIFESTATION AND THE MISSION

*I*n this chapter, we will help coalesce the work we have been doing in order to create a viable plan to shift our energy into alignment with the Highest available to us, toward Re-membering soul and mission.

But first, let's take a look at ***manifestation,*** an element of all mission and purpose, all project and plan fulfillment.

Manifestation—Human, Soul, Angelic

Manifestation is a word that has both a human/vernacular meaning and a Divine Soul/esoteric one. We are interested in each of those meanings here.

Human Level of Manifestation

On the human, earthly level, the word manifestation comes from Latin roots meaning "visible, clear or apparent." We will be looking for visible, palpable results: our creation through our actions will have consequences that will be clear and tangible. In a grounded way, through action, we move toward our soul mission.

Example: John manifested a love of music by taking guitar and singing lessons and practicing.

Soul/Divine Level of Manifestation

The soul or Divine level of manifestation is supported in two main ways: working with our Divine aspect, our soul, and our invisible Friends in High Places, the Angels.

Soul

As we align with our soul, our power increases, and manifestation becomes at once more fluid and more subtle. We begin to understand, and then see evidence of, the fact that we create not only through our actions but also through our words, thoughts, and emotions; that is, we create energetically. We are energetic beings living in human form, and this becomes more and more clear. We are much more powerful that anyone ever told us. In an energetic way, we step into our power and create tangible results, but through Divine, energetic means.

Example: John worked to manifest his secret dream of playing music and having a singing career by doing regular visualizations, creating an energy field around him to help attract his dream.

Angels

Although we can do this work on our own (children of Creator, we are powerful, and we create), why not access the help that is already on hand, as we have seen? Why not, for example, ask the Angels around us, or, depending on the creation we have in mind, the relevant Archangels?

Example: He asked Archangel Sandalphon to accompany him in his dream of playing music and singing.

Both Human and Soul Level of Manifestation: Re-membering

When we awaken to Who We Are, Truly and realize that we indeed have a soul and a mission, often we want to jump in and get to it! For this, it behooves us to move our vehicle (us) forward on all cylinders; that is, by taking tangible, human action and working on an energetic level, stepping into our Divine power, and asking for Angelic assistance, all in one!

Example: It was so important to John to manifest his dreams that, even as he took music lessons and practiced, he also worked energetically with visualizations, and at the same time called on his Guardian Angels and Archangel Sandalphon (Music of God) to assist and direct him, knowing that his desire was Divinely inspired.

This book is about understanding the soul mission manifestation process (Re-membering or aligning our free will and life purpose to our soul mission), as well as setting out a plan and a mission statement that will help us move tangibly in that direction.

As we move into the planning piece of our time together, it is important to bring all aspects to bear on our journey: human manifestation, soul manifestation, and manifestation with Angelic assistance!

But before we begin to work on the plan, let us delve more deeply into each of these aspects.

Human Manifestation through Action

On a human level, everyone knows that actions have consequences. If we want to get something done, achieve a purpose, we need to get out from under our blanket fort, and take action!

But what kind of action should we take? At what cadence (fast? slow?)? How should we proceed?

As we begin to put a plan in place, it will be important to ensure that each step is:

- *exciting*, but not too scary (the *Eek-Yay!* Effect)
- *clear and concise* as to "what" and "when," and thus, actionable
- *easy to achieve* (baby steps!)
- *able to be undertaken under our own power* (not dependent on someone else)
- fun!

We will apply these standards to each step we put in place in our plans, so let us look at these points here now, noting that they are important for the plan we will work on here, but also for all manifestation steps, for the success of any project.

Standards/Techniques for Manifestation Steps
Each of our planned steps should meet the fabulous five criteria noted above, as follows:

1 The Eek-Yay! Effect—
A manifestation step should be exciting, but not too scary
The step we put into place should not be so scary it makes us sick or immobilizes us. Sounds obvious, right? And yet, we humans, once we get

hot on a subject, often overdo it, trying to go too fast, as if making up for lost time.

The idea is certainly not to scare the wits out of the tender, talented child within us, who we need on our side, by brusquely (violently?) pushing them out of their comfort zone/blanket fort, but rather, to take things one step at a time at a rhythm that is more fun and exciting than scary: the afore-mentioned *Eek-Yay!* Effect.

The *Eek-Yay!* Effect occurs when we, as humans, experience the pump as primed for change, and the change we are contemplating is exactly what is called for: there is both *eek!* and *yay!*—nervous energy but also delight.

There is *eek!* because we are stepping out of our blanket forts, and that is always exciting and a wee bit scary—but only a wee bit! We should not be frightened into immobility; we should not be so scared that we puke. We should not have to force ourselves to move forward!

The world teaches us (through school and work experiences, among others) that sometimes we need to force ourselves, but when we are working on manifestation, forcing anything is *not* recommended. Why? Because when we force ourselves, the energy is fear not Love, despair not Joy. You get the idea!

Of course, that does not mean we drop our desire; rather, it is suggested that we simply reduce the size of the step in front of us, so that we feel curiosity and desire about it instead of anguish.

Remember: A little fear is normal, but just a little: an *eek!* should be largely outshone by a *yay!* There needs to be *yay!* There needs to be Joy and delight in moving forward toward the soul mission. With compassion, notice when the *eek!* appears. There is always a bit of an *eek!* when we step out from under the covers, but concentrating on the *yay!* will dissipate it, in line with the Universal Law of Energy we have already seen: "Where our attention goes, so goes our energy."

The step descriptions that follow will help us to keep the fear level down and the happiness level up.

2 A manifestation step should be clear and concise (what, when, and how) and thus, actionable

Think of the first job you ever had. How nervous you might have been, at least until you got the hang of things: how the lady liked her tea, or the games the kids liked to play, how the fryer or cash register or lawn mower worked. Perhaps you can remember noticing then that your level of ease increased as you understood what was required of you and your ability to meet those requirements.

Now, think of the last time you were new at something and things were not clear to you—what to do at a job, perhaps? Or how to behave in a new relationship or club? Or how to get the garbage hauled and other rules of living when moving to a new town? In these situations, were you at ease? More to the point here, were you Joyful?

I am betting the answer is no, since as humans, our Joy is related to feeling peaceful in a space, and when we do not know what is expected of us, we are not in that energy at all.

For this reason, the second rule for manifestation steps is to be *very specific* as to who, what, and where, so that there is clarity and we can relax into the challenges we have before us with more *yay* than ever!

Example: I will practice singing "To Dream the Impossible Dream" every Tuesday evening for 15 minutes, whether I am at home or for some reason elsewhere.

This step is very precise action (as to time and place and action), and so is of optimal clarity.

3 A manifestation step should be easy to achieve!!!

There are three exclamation points after this one because it is really, really, really important!

I know, if you are (like me) a bit Type A and used to setting the bar high in your earthly adventures, this might be a tough one, but that is precisely why it is so important, and not just to overachievers!

Think of a situation where someone you know (or maybe you), set the bar too high in life: a deadline too short, perhaps; a physical, mental, or emotional task too great.

How did that go for you: was there success? If so, was it Joyful?

Probably not. If we set the bar too high, even if we leap tall buildings and manage to get it done, we often will arrive at the finish completely spent, maybe hurt, and perhaps useless for anything afterward for a while (my last marathon comes to mind). And that's *if* we succeed!!

Now imagine the (more likely) scenario of failure: We set the bar too high, life got in the way (as it always does), and we fell short of our goal. How did that feel? Not good at all, am I right? Furthermore, each time we fail along the path of life, it erodes our confidence in ourselves a bit more, until that blanket fort starts looking better and better!

Solution: In order to avoid the trap of setting the bar too high, we will do just the opposite: **Set the bar way too low—ridiculously low, even!**

That's right, you heard me! I did not say to set it reasonably high or reasonably low, but *ridiculously* low. Why?

When we are playing the game of inner energy and confidence in ourselves, each time we set the bar and we achieve it (whether it was set "high" or "low"), we get a shot of confidence. And when we set it very low, we have extra energy after meeting our goal, so we will perhaps even surpass the goal that was set, making us feel even more a winner! Even if we are aware of all this, each time we get to check the box of a task we committed to complete—or, hallelujah, surpassed!—it works energetically. We feel better and better about ourselves, which greases the wheels of our vehicles for the Great Shining to come. Success breeds success, in line with the famous "Energy seeks equilibrium." So, ensure your success by ensuring your steps for success!

4 A manifestation step should be possible on our own, not dependent on others

While I am all for teamwork, for the purposes of aligning with our soul mission, this needs to be a solo mission. Our mission may support a group movement, but our plan needs to be independent of the free will of others. We can, of course, as we shall examine in a bit, call on our Angels for help, but in creating our plan to shift and align our purpose with our soul mission, we need to create a plan that does not depend on another human being.

For example, a good manifestation step would not be to sign a manager for our music career, but rather it could be to look for a manager to help our career. See the difference?

A manifestation step must recognize the rules of the Game, so we need to be aware of the free will of others. We cannot know if the people we contact will say yes; of course they might, but maybe the soul plan is for someone else to step up, and we cannot know that. Since it is not clear, it contradicts rule number 2: the clear and concise requirement.

When we create our plan, we build in steps that optimize the likelihood of finding partners who will support our journey (I call them "cheerleaders," and we will look at that in the next section, exploring the process of manifestation energetically on a soul level). But we cannot include anything that will depend on the free-will choice of another person in our plan. Again, this is to ensure that the plan be **independently doable,** bringing us back to the points above.

5 A manifestation step should be fun

This step may seem frivolous (or fun!), but it is not. Even the best of intentions set at New Year's will fall by the wayside (maybe by March . . . or January 5) if we are not enjoying the activity. When we choose steps that will be both fun and bring us in the direction of our mission, we again set the stage for success.

Additionally, the more we enjoy something, the more Joy, Light, and Love is in our energetic field, which as we know attracts our experience. So light up with fun!

Soul Manifestation through Energy

We just looked at manifestation through the human level, through actions; however, we know that action is not the only way we create, don't we?

Once we break free of the limiting belief that action is the only way to change things, we can open more to the power of manifestation through energy, which aligns us with the creative power of our soul through Source.

Here, too, we will rely on two Universal Laws of Energy we have been looking at all along:

- "Energy seeks equilibrium."
- "Where our attention goes, so goes energy."

Specifically, we will recognize the image we discussed earlier: We each have an energetic field around us.

We know this to be true, don't we? Just think of the last time someone was standing behind you and you felt their presence, even though they did not touch you and you did not see them. This happened because their energetic field was impacting yours.

Further, maybe you have a memory that when you felt the impact of the energetic field of the other person, it was either a "good" experience or a "bad" one, pleasant or unpleasant.

If that is the case, you are likely a "sensitive," as noticing whether it feels good or not to be in someone's field or having them in ours is an aspect of clairsentience, a form of clairvoyance. At any rate, if you did feel that way, it makes sense. When the person is in resonance with our energy, their presence will feel congruous and agreeable, and when they are not in harmony with our energy, it might feel negative, disagreeable, maybe even make us want to move away.

This is entirely in alignment with the first Law of Energy above: "Energy seeks equilibrium." (For more information on energetic interactions and how to master your vehicle/energy, all is explained in my book, *Inviting Angels into Your Life*.)

Techniques for Manifestation Steps with Energy

Each of our planned steps will take the form of energetic creation: Words, Thoughts, and Emotions. Each one we will now explore invites us to shift and change our energetic field in order to shift and change what we attract in service to our mission. This is foundational work. Our understanding of this will help us to be more effective in including energetic manifestation techniques such as visualizations in the mission plans we are preparing to create.

Words for Soul Manifestation

"You are stupid!" or "You are so smart!"

"Such a handsome boy / lovely girl!" or *"You are so ugly. Get out of my sight!"*

"I know you can do it!" or *"Are you sure you have it in you?"*

The above are all examples—positive or negative—of words that a child might hear growing up in the world. Some are extreme examples, perhaps, but life gives us all innumerable examples, all of which are pertinent here. We can imagine many variations, positively impacting the hearer or not, such as "The world doesn't work that way, princess" or, simply, "I'm proud of you."

What phrases impacted you?

Each phrase (even in the reading or the writing of it) impacts us, because words and phrases carry energy. They carry the energy of intention, which (as we know) creates, but when we put words on an intention (consciously or unconsciously), our creation is strengthened. It is logical, isn't it?

We focus on a preexisting idea in order to speak words to communicate it, and where our attention goes/is focused, well, you know, we create!

In fact, every time we speak, the energy that creates worlds issues forth from us! This is why cultivating the capacity for and tendency to silence is a great way to strengthen ourselves energetically. Each word we utter carries with it such power, and so, lessens the energy within. How often are our words wasted? How often do we create with our words unconsciously?

This is also why people who talk a lot don't seem to be particularly powerful people, right? As they speak to us, perhaps our eyes glaze over, or our thoughts stray to our shopping list? On the other hand, a "strong, silent type" is a type for a reason. Such people speak rarely, but when they do, we want to listen! Their silence is part of their strength.

Now, let's go back to the phrases above. Each one can uplift or cut down, and that is when others project them at us! Now, imagine how much more powerful is the impact of both compliment and diatribe when it is directed toward ourselves!

Do not use your words to play small; playing small creates small!

Maintaining a high energetic is important when we are speaking to creation. Words in phrases like "at any rate, it will never work," or "it's just a silly dream" (it's not!) are phrases we may be in the habit of throwing around so folks around us don't find us uppity, or they may be things we say to ourselves so as not to be disappointed if things don't work out (creating the idea that they won't work out).

Seriously, who cares (really!) what others think? This is not their life, but yours! What do they know of your hopes, dreams, and your mission?

At this point in history, when we have moved out of survival as priority, many of us are waking up and beginning to suspect that there is more, that we have a mission. Still, most of us are still so preoccupied with the business of just getting along, that we are not at all aware of, and have no time for, any conscious soul mission-ing.

When we step out of our comfort zone, when we cease playing small and take steps toward our soul dream, our actions may create discomfort in others. Remember the canoe image, and imagine yourself and each person you know in an energetic equilibrium (Universal Law of Energy). No, in a shared energetic canoe with you, one that is stable as long as no one moves around too much. So what happens if you stand up? When we take steps to grow and evolve, it can shake up the ones we love.

Well, so what? Or rather, great! Instead of deciding not to grow to avoid making those around us uncomfortable, imagine that we are in a soul contract with each of them, and we are *meant* to be the alarm that is going off, annoying but perhaps awakening them!

The people who are around us when we shift and change are never there by accident. These are all soul contracts, which are meant to give the other soul the possibility of "drafting" as a result of our shifting, maybe allowing them to awaken midstream on their path.

A Lightworker is not meant to be like everybody else. Our energy *should* shake things up; our Light becoming stronger and stronger, until just being around us will create a space where awakening is possible.

What other human beings around us do with that space is up to them, but it is ours to be loyal to our vessel, to respect our path, no matter what they choose to do. Some will run away, preferring the comfort (if boredom) of their blanket fort. Others will stir and awaken, coming along for the ride. If this speaks to you at all, it is quite likely that waking up, and then waking others up is part of your path, your soul mission.

Using words with precision, knowing that each word has an impact and not allowing what others think or say to impact us, is important as it can help us consciously use words as steps to manifestation. When we become accustomed to the power of our words, we may be (even more) attracted to do work with affirmations and visualizations to facilitate manifestations.

A final important point here is remembering that the child within you—the one with the key to your creativity and Joy—is listening! The words you use will have a positive or negative impact on your energy, inside and out. Become the adult the child within you can count on to always be their cheerleader. There are enough critics in the world. Don't be one of them! Don't tear down your creation before it can even be made manifest.

This is not just important for our words but also for our thoughts, which we will look at next.

Thought for Soul Manifestation

We have been told that we create with our words, and have just seen that, indeed, words can create an impact in the world in a very tangible way. In a more subtle way, we can say the same for thoughts.

The thoughts of others are none of your business!

The main point here is that we cannot control the thoughts of others (free will, and all that!). But it is known that the thoughts of others do impact us, and not only when they take shape in words or actions. When someone is thinking strongly about us, sometimes it triggers a reaction; it has a tangible effect. Have you never had an experience like the following?

Telephone rings or email or text arrives: "*Wow, hello! That's so funny. I was just thinking about you!*"

In fact, this is not "funny" at all, but normal . . . on an energetic or soul level. Every thought we have travels to the person we think about and impacts their energetic field!

Wow, imagine that! Even the secret thoughts we would never want to see the light of day, see, in a way, the light of day! It would have been good to get the manual that should have come with this body of ours, *non*? But now we know, no matter that no one ever told us, and no sense crying over the spilled milk of thoughts of the past! But from here and now, let's be mindful and responsible, conscious about what we create, minding every thought!

This energetic truth ("Where our attention goes, so goes the energy that creates") means that every nice thought we have for someone (or even ourselves) is like an energetic boon, an energy hug, if you will. On the other hand, every negative thought is an energy arrow, piercing and creating a hole in the field of the other, which can leak energy.

Even any form of fantasy around someone is kind of like black magic: we are interfering in a person's energy field without their permission. Of course, it is not really "black magic," because we are not doing it intentionally, but it will have an impact on the person, nonetheless (it is not because we don't hit someone with our vehicle intentionally that they will not be harmed).

As our sensitivity/clairsentience becomes clearer, we can see or feel or simply know that this impact is real, so we get clear that it is not right to behave in such irresponsible ways. By not respecting the free will of the other person, we create karma for ourselves. But that, perhaps, is for another book . . .

For our purposes here, when we step into our power and consciously decide to align our human purpose with our soul mission, it is important to recognize the power of our thoughts, on others and on ourselves. Negative thoughts or "stinkin' thinkin'," and positive, uplifting thoughts have two very different impacts on our energy field, and thus, directly limit what we can experience in the Earth field. We only experience what is in resonance with our field at any given time, except when it is a wake-up call or a soul marker experience that shifts our energy in the moment (like the smack of a shaman or the Angel gifting me with a crystal at the bank).

Our thoughts are important, not only for the effect they have on our field but also for the effect they have on our emotions, which carry a potency in manifestation.

 Exercise

EMOTIONS FOR SOUL MANIFESTATION

This fun exercise uses two different ways of saying the same sentence.

First, simply read this phrase out loud, "I feel good today."

Now, close your eyes, and remember a time (maybe right now?) when you felt really, really good. Breathe it in BIG, feel it!

Then, on the out-breath, with a sweeping breath, sweep that good-ness into all the cells of your body, all levels of your being.

Now, with all of that energy, say again, "I feel good today!"

Notice the difference?

Our words and thoughts create, but the potency of the energy that fills our energetic field is related to how those words and thoughts make us feel! Every emotion is rooted in a thought. Every. Single. One. Conversely, our emotions also color our words and thoughts. It's all tied up together.

This means that when we are happy, our thoughts and words align with that emotion, and together our fields are filled with good, so we attract the good. But it also means that when we are *not* happy, our thoughts and words align with that emotion, and together our fields are filled with nega-tivity, so we attract the negative.

The beauty of this understanding, however, is this: When we know that an emotion is always tied to a thought, we can better manage our instru-ment. When we are feeling pulled downward and out of our sweet spot, we can simply identify the thought behind it and *place our attention, and so, our energy, on a different thought.* This works powerfully; I have been working with it for a time now, and highly recommend it!

Contrary to what happens in unconscious experience, we are not neces-sarily subject to our emotions; we can consciously take over the wheel of our vehicle and drive our experience, benefitting from such foundational understandings of manifestation on the Divine or energetic level as the two salient facts here: that our emotions are powerful influencers of our experience, and that they can be changed by shifting our underlying thinking.

EXAMPLE: Change of Perspective

One day, I was sad because I was not able to be in the United States when my first English language book, *Inviting Angels into Your Life*, came out. I was wallowing a bit, truth be told, feeling like I had just had a baby but wasn't able to hold it. But I didn't let that feeling last long! (These days, I pay attention to what is going on with my vehicle.) I recognized the thought that was making me sad, and thus, shifted my perspective and focused (knowing that where my attention goes, so goes my energy) instead on the fact that having a book come out in English was the realization of a dream since I was a child. Presto, change-o! I am sure that if a clairvoyant had been next to me, they would have seen my energetic field positively light up with the shift!

We have explored both human manifestation practices through action, and Divine/soul manifestation practices through words, thoughts, and emotions. Now, we will look at another aspect of Divine manifestation: help from the Angels!

Manifestation through Asking for (and Accepting) Help

Basically, whether we recognize it or not, there are only two ways we advance in life: by free will or by intuition or guidance.

Free will is when we, on a human level, decide what we want to do, where we want to go. We have already explored ways in which we can use our free will to create, with actions, words, thoughts, and emotions.

Guidance, or intuition, is the alternative. This way of going forward sees us sometimes doing things that lead others to shake their heads, befuddled. We may even surprise ourselves, noticing that there is no apparent logic behind our decisions. Of course, even in intuitive situations, we use our free will to undertake the actions pursuant to the guidance received; there is always choice. But there is an element of otherworldliness that comes into play here, where we intuit our next steps; we feel (clairsentience), see (clairvoyance), hear (clairaudience,) or simply know (claircognizance, or intuition) the way to go. When we decide to invite the Angels into our planning and execution of Re-membering (which is always a good idea), we are tending toward this second way of living and of moving forward.

We have already talked a good bit about **who** the Angels are, and which Archangels might help us with which activities. Now, let's focus on the **how** of our collaboration with the Angels, using actions and energy and words, thoughts, and emotions.

Asking for Help

If we are to receive help from the Angels, as we know, we need to ask. They will only intervene if we ask, unless there is a situation of mortal risk, and then, only if it is not our time to die.

Often from clients I hear two stumbling blocks to asking: first, not being in the habit of asking for help, and second, not knowing how to ask. Let's look at both.

The Habit of Accepting Help

Sometimes our experience on Earth may have taught us, from a young age, that it doesn't make sense to ask for help because no one can be depended upon. Perhaps others have disappointed us, and we fell out of the habit of asking, preferring to go it on our own.

This is sadly often the case for Lightworkers, as such souls are often evolved and thus, their human expression is fairly capable at getting along in life. When that is the case, it bolsters the tendency to go it alone if our experience proves others unreliable, as described above. For such people, *giving is often much easier than receiving,* mainly because habits have formed. But this disequilibrium of giving more than you get, while thought to be altruistic, is actually not good for our energy bodies, and so, not good for our soul mission.

Learning to ask can be tripped up by pride and fear of refusal, and our past experiences, even forgotten ones, color our perceptions. The beauty of working with Angels on this is that they can help us heal and transform the limiting belief that no one will help.

Angels will always help. Always! They will never let us down. So any fear of being disappointed or disrespected after having opened up in vulnerability to ask for help is a non-issue with the Angels.

Accepting help from Angels has the advantage, then, of creating more confidence and balance between what we give and what we receive in our life experience, creating harmony and confidence. This can allow us to eventually open up to other human beings, perhaps ones sent by Angels at first, like the woman in the bank with the amethyst crystal. We can even ask the Angels to help us in asking them for help!

Let's now take a look at the second block to asking and receiving help from the Angels on our soul mission: Not knowing how to ask and learning **how** to go about it.

Clairvoyance: Language of the Angels

Because I have the great fortune to do the work I do, I often meet people who ask me how they can best communicate with Angels. My answer is always, basically, the same: with authenticity and from the heart.

We do not need elaborate ceremonies: The Angels do not stand on formality; we humans do. And while I do so love the church rituals of my Christian culture, beautiful psalms and prayers and singing choirs, I know also that all the pomp and ceremony is for us; neither God nor the Angels have any need of it. Ritual helps us focus our attention and thus, our creative energy in support of our intention. The Angels, operating from Unity, have no such need of focus.

Rituals elevate our energy and facilitate communication, but the Angels of God are already here with us, ready to communicate; they are just waiting for us to catch up and catch on! When we do, we can begin to communicate with them very simply, from our heart to them, and from them through our instruments to our heart.

Often I hear, "Kathryn, I talk to my Angels all the time; they never answer," to which I respond, "Yes they do. You just don't hear the answer."

While we send messages to the Angels with our words and thoughts and feelings, we can note here that the Angels can read our hearts and know our needs before even we do. So that side of communicating, from us to them, is covered!

But on the receiving side, The Forgetting and ensuing walls built up for self-protection against the harshness of the world sadly also block our clairvoyance, our capacity to receive their guidance, making it harder to communicate and collaborate in manifestation with them. I wrote a whole book on this, *Inviting Angels into Your Life,* but it is worth highlighting here the aspects of Angelic communication through our clairvoyant gifts to facilitate manifestation:

Your Clairvoyant Gifts

You are likely already aware that you have clairvoyant gifts. We all do. Whether we use these gifts actively or they lie dormant, each of us has clairvoyant capacities which, if utilized, can facilitate accepting assistance from the Angels.

Looking at the body as an instrument, most of us are aware that the majority of us "play" the Game with five senses that help us move through life. What is less known is that, complementing these five human senses are four energetic/Divine ones, and it is through these that we can most easily understand what the Angels are trying to tell us.

The Angels communicate with us by playing our instrument, in a sense: by sending us visuals we see (clairvoyance) or messages we hear (clairaudience) or experiences we feel (clairsentience) or simply by conjoining their understanding with ours (claircognizance, or intuition). Our five senses are important in this, as it is through our body and its senses that we communicate with the Angels, and indeed, all that is beyond the veil, including our soul.

Types of Clairvoyance

In the large sense, clairvoyance is defined as "a capacity to see/understand things in an extraordinary way, over and above what is deemed 'normal.'"

In our clairvoyant experience, we "see" or "get" something that someone else standing right next to us might not "see" or "get" at all.

Even if we have never had a clairvoyant experience until now, this gift is waiting for us all, and the Angels can help us open it! As with any talent or gift, we cultivate it through practice, and by communicating regularly with the Angels, and accepting their help, we can advance toward our soul mission and develop these capacities quite easily.

The "extra-ordinary" understanding that is clairvoyance can be expressed in four different ways: first, in a way that is also called *clairvoyance,* or clear sight, as well as *clairaudience,* or clear hearing; *clairsentience,* or clear feeling; *and claircognizance,* or clear knowing or intuition.

Let's take a closer look.

Clairvoyance is defined here as "the capacity to see images that allow us to understand things in an extraordinary way." This includes capacities that might appear unique or rare (even odd), where human beings like you and I see dead people or auras or Angels, etcetera. Such seeing may be experienced with our actual eyes, though that form is rarer. As dreams also include images, clairvoyant dreaming is included in this category of gift. Most often, we "see" on the "inner screen" we all have, but don't always recognize:

Example: Close your eyes, and think of the face of someone you love. Think of their eyes, their nose, their lips, and their mouth. See them smile at you.

There! That is the inner screen of clairvoyance on which we may receive flashes or visions offered by the Angels to help us understand something important for our path.

But there are other ways that Angels may communicate with us through clairvoyance: Anything that is a message that our instrument captures which includes an image is clairvoyance.

EXAMPLE: Clear-Sightedness

At one point along my path, I was trying to decide if I should go to Brazil to participate in a Manna teacher training, to allow me to accompany others in activating our capacity to feed ourselves with energy. While I felt called to go, my logical side was concerned because it was expensive and long and on the other side of the planet. So one morning, I decided to ask my Angels. I opened my channel (just as we have learned to do here), and when I connected to Source and soul and the Angels, I asked them if it was in my Highest and best interests to go to Brazil for the training. And then I got ready for my day. When I left my apartment building a half-hour later, a bus was passing. I looked up, and on the side of the bus was a billboard with one word: YES! (The fact that it was YES and not OUI, even though I live in France, was the pièce de resistance.) I went to Brazil, and am so glad I did!

We have seen a practical way in which, through using clairvoyance, the Angels can help us on our path. Now let's look at clairaudience.

Clairaudience is defined here as "the capacity to hear or understand beyond the norm by means of sound." This includes what I would call the Hollywood version of clairaudience we see on TV or in the movies: a medium hearing messages from the dead or from the Angels. But it also includes hearing anything that helps us understand what the Angels are trying to communicate. This can be words we hear from them directly, either in a dream or awake, but also music lyrics, snippets of conversation we "happen" to hear (remember, there are no accidents!), and things that other people might "randomly" say to us.

Any person who bridges the worlds, who acts as intermediary between our physical world and the invisible is acting as a medium, an intermediary . . . even when we do it for ourselves. We may hear with our actual ears or (most often) with our inner hearing.

I find most often that the difference between a person who benefits from inner hearing/clairaudience and one who does not, is not so much whether or not they have a gift, but whether or not they are *aware* of that gift. We cannot utilize or cultivate a talent we do not even know we have! Thus, opening up to our inner hearing is an essential step on the path.

Exercise
INNER HEARING

Close your eyes (closing our eyes to hear better is effective as it allows for less "input" and thus, fewer distractions and a concentration that will be both more subtle and more powerful). Now, imagine the person in the exercise above, or someone else you care for very much. Concentrate on that person until you can remember their voice, maybe something they would often say, or the sounds of their laughter or singing (or yelling—whatever works). In this way, use your imagination to "hear" their voice or a sound you associate with them. As we do so, this connects us directly with the person, whether they are still alive or not.

Our inner hearing can be cultivated by doing such exercises. Like a muscle, the more we use it, the more access we have to that capacity, and the more our inner hearing becomes available to us—not just facilitating "recall" exercises but, over time, as a way to receive messages from our Angels, Guides, or loved ones.

As we begin to notice what sounds are going on for us internally, we may notice songs that "pop" into our head, or key phrases that seem to crop up in a repetitive manner. This kind of clariaudience can happen either in the ESP (Hollywood) way or in a much more down-to-earth way: imagine a car passing by, windows open, and suddenly a song spills out. Instantly, our body reacts: hair stands on end, or our eyes fill with tears . . . This is a typical and extraordinarily ordinary experience of clairaudience.

As with clairvoyance, the more we work on/pay attention to the sounds around us or exercise our will to hear with the inner ear (using exercises like the one above), the more we flex our clairaudient muscles and open up to our clairaudient gifts.

EXAMPLE:
Angel Messages through Clairaudience

When I started to open wide and actively engage with my Angels, I was still a banker, but I had had enough and was getting ready to quit; that is, until I heard an Angelic message: "Wait a year!" I didn't know why, but right away I knew who was telling me to wait, so I decided I would. During the year that followed, the bank I worked for decided to change strategies and recall many expatriates to the United States from overseas. In recalling me from Paris, they broke my contract. Since I did not quit (thank you, Angels), I was freed up to do what I desired, but with a payoff that allowed me the freedom to explore the spiritual world full time.

As you can see from the above example, requesting Angelic help is not just a heavenly, airy-fairy idea; there is very earthly benefit! But clairaudience is not the only way they can tangibly help us when we ask the Angels for help with our mission. There is also clairsentience . . .

Clairsentience is defined as "the capacity to know and understand things through the feelings of our bodies, including our senses of touch, smell, and taste." We have already talked about our energy field, and each of us experiences perhaps daily the impact of clairsentience, if we pay attention.

"I have a feeling . . . "

What do we feel?

Perhaps we walk into a room and feel welcome (or not), or uncomfortable in certain spaces (a hospital, a cemetery) and, conversely, great in others (at a friend's house, at church, in our favorite place in nature, or a spa?). The difference between these places, which logically should not have an impact on our sense of well-being, is the energy.

Clairsentience is all about the energy.

Each instrument plays differently, and, if we ask, the presence of Angels around us helps us discover how to play ours.

Ever had goosebumps? If you have, then you probably know, if you think about it, that there are "good" goosebumps and there are "bad" goosebumps, right? "Good" goosebumps happen when something wonderful occurs; they accompany feelings of Joy and peace. "Bad" goosebumps, however, bring neither Joy nor peace, but rather anguish and foreboding. In both cases, the same physical phenomenon occurs, but instinctively we know which is "bad" and which "good." This means that *we already instinctively know how to play our instruments!*

The Angels can use our capacity to feel energy by sending us good goosebumps for a yes, or bad ones in warning. They also can flood our body with warmth, bring tears to our eyes, or brush our skin with their feathers. Generally, though each of our instruments plays differently, when Angels are around it feels good!

Other, less common, ways clairsentience can be experienced are through our senses of **taste** and **smell**. We may experience a taste in our mouth which is illogical, maybe Grandma's cookies (though she may be deceased, and though we are not eating at that moment). Even more prevalent are instances where people experience through their sense of smell: an odor we detect (pipe, perfume, baking, aftershave) when there is no "logical" source. The taste and smell forms of clairvoyance are more rare but no less valid, and can be very comforting reminders of a loved one who has passed.

EXAMPLE:
Angel Message through Clairsentience

One way in which my instrument plays is through tears. At the beginning of my path, it was unnerving, because I was taught not to cry as a child and thus wasn't comfortable with it. But later, especially when I learned that St. Francis of Assisi and St. Clare would sometimes pray together in tears, I understood that tears can mark and honor sacred experience. When I really feel the Angels, I feel the love of God, not just for me but for all of us. The compassion, tenderness, and gentle understanding that is there flows as if in a flood of Love. And every time, it makes me cry. My instrument reacts to Divine Presence most often through tears, a form of clairsentient experience. Also, when I do individual sessions, communicating Angel messages to people who come to me, when I am spot on, when I have transmitted an Angelic response particularly clearly, they flood warmth through my being in what I call a whoosh!, from above to below. And I always say thank you! (Expressing gratitude in this way also makes communication more fluid.)

A final way Angels work with us is through claircognizance, or intuition.

Claircognizance is defined here as "clear inner knowing. Also called intuition, this is revealed at those times when we just know. We don't know how we know, but we know!"

The telephone rings, and you "know" who it is. Or a friend talks about an interview they went on, and you "know" that they'll get the job.

Angels will work with our claircognizance in response to questions we pose, guidance we request. We might see, hear or feel the answer, or we might simply wake up knowing the answer.

EXAMPLE:
Claircognizance and the Angels

Some years ago, I walked the Camino, a 500-mile pilgrimage from the South of France across the north of Spain to the cathedral Santiago de Compostela, where St. James (Santiago) is buried. About halfway along, I was hurting and my feet were pretty banged up. Before going to sleep that night (which is often how I work with the Angels), I asked them if I should continue or go home, then I went to sleep. I awoke with the idea of Archangel Raguel in my head. Raguel (as I teach students) helps us by boosting our energy, among other things. I had forgotten all about asking for help! I understood the message and kept walking, never forgetting to ask Raguel for help again. I finished the pilgrimage in good form and thanked the Angels in general, and Archangel Raguel in particular, for their accompaniment and aid.

Claircognizance specifically, and clairvoyance overall, is quite helpful in receiving messages from the Angels on our path to fulfilling our soul mission . . . when we listen to it! Of course, in this, too, we have free will, but it is always a good idea both to ask the Angels for help *and* to accept their help and guidance.

Now that our understanding and preparation are complete, we are ready for next steps toward discovering and putting in place a plan to realize our individual soul mission. In the next chapter, we will look at the mechanism of manifestation from an energetic perspective and work on our plan to align with soul for our mission . . . with help from the Angels!

Chapter 11

THE MISSION MANIFESTATION PLAN

*B*efore we begin our work on the Mission Manifestation Plan, let's take a look at something that will help us become excellent mission manifesters: how manifestation works energetically.

For this, we will look closely at the main energy centers that drive our energy body, our Divine aspect—the chakras and their manifestation role.

The Chakras of Manifestation

The image below gives a rudimentary understanding of the chakra system. Here, we will focus on the impact of each chakra on the process of the manifestation of each step toward our soul sweet spots and finding fulfillment in our mission.

The process of manifestation begins (no surprise) with inspiration from above, and descends to be manifested on Earth through our energy body, chakra by chakra, in a process we unknowingly repeat with each action we manifest, with each idea "baby" we birth.

The steps described below the image happen unconsciously, for the most part, but why not render the process conscious in order to help it along and ask the Angels or Archangels for help in this?

For each step in the process, we will look at the role the chakra plays in creation and a practical example of how that happens, along with the Archangel we might want to ask to assist with that part of manifestation. As you look at this process, think of something you have already created, to see if or how these steps occurred for you.

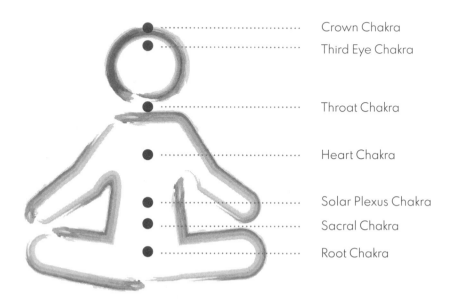

Crown Chakra
Third Eye Chakra
Throat Chakra
Heart Chakra
Solar Plexus Chakra
Sacral Chakra
Root Chakra

Chakras and Soul Mission

For those not familiar with the chakra system, here is a brief explanation.

Imagine the human body as we see it in the biology books, with its system of veins, the blood highways that carry nourishment to our cells and carry away waste from them. Now, imagine our energy body. It also has "veins," known as *meridians,* which carry energy throughout our body, both filling and emptying, and for the most part we are not conscious of either process. We can find a map of the meridians as easily as we can find a map of the blood vessels throughout the physical body; a quick search online will do the trick.

Half the people on the planet recognize the meridians and the energetic system as the foundation of human health and base their system of medicine on it. The lines of acupuncture and acupressure fall along these lines. The more fluid the energy flowing through our energy body, the better our health and well-being will be on all levels: physical, mental, emotional, and spiritual/energetic.

When it comes to our soul mission, this is also true: the better the energy flow through our meridians and chakras, and the better care we take of that energy, the more easily we find ourself in alignment with our soul, and the more easily our channel will be open and clear, allowing Angels to support our mission. For this reason, we look at this all-important energy system here, specifically with regard to manifestation and soul mission.

Anywhere the meridian lines cross is a crossroad, or *chakra*, which have been described as wheels of energy. There are seven primary chakras in the body, where many lines cross. They begin at the root chakra, between our legs, and continue to the top of our head, the crown chakra (this placement of the seven primary chakras comes as no surprise to those of us who recognize that the energy channel between Earth and Sky travels vertically along the spinal column).

Each chakra is said to contribute (or not, depending on if it is blocked or open) to the fluidity of an important aspect of our lives and fulfillment of our soul mission! Below, we explore the process of manifestation by looking at the contribution of each chakra as we take each step to create and fulfill our soul mission.

At the end of each step, I will share an example of that step as it occurred with regard to the manifestation of a part of my own soul mission: the writing of this book. As ever, this is done to make sure the steps are clear for your own manifestations to come!

The Process of Manifestation from an Energetic Point of View

Crown Chakra

The Crown chakra is the energetic link between our human being-ness and our Divine being-ness, the soul that expresses Source. The more aligned with our soul we consciously become, the clearer it is that inspiration comes from above, from the Divine, from our soul level, sometimes through the guidance of Angels.

The Crown chakra is located where the anterior (front) fontanelle, or the easily perceived soft spot at the top of the head, is located. It is the last part of our skull to close, contributing to and completing The Forgetting early in life.

As we undertake practices like those included in this book to open our clairvoyant gifts and align with our purpose in coming here, this chakra opens more and more, and we Re-remember. The more open this chakra is, the more aligned we are to our soul and thus, to our mission.

Our Guardian Angels and Archangel Raziel can help us in this. Inviting our Guardian Presence along with us is always a good idea, as that is why they exist. Archangel Raziel is suggested for this piece of the manifestation puzzle, as He is the Archangel most closely connected with our soul, or Divine Truth. He can assist with this part of the process, keeping the gate to the heavens open, the chakra fluid, and helping the embodiment (incarnation) of our soul, and thus, our mission.

Manifestation Example: As a step toward my soul mission, the inspiration for this book came to me through the crown chakra. Thank you, Angels!

Third Eye Chakra

Our Third Eye Chakra is our seat of clairvoyance and understanding—how we see the world. As such, it is an important step in the process. At this step in the manifestation process, we think about the inspiration we have received. Our inspiration "baby" becomes a budding project, and it is still ours alone. As we become aware of the idea, and think about it, we add energy to creation ("Where our attention goes, so goes the energy that creates"). As we reflect on it, it begins to take on a clearer form for us, and it is formed on the energetic level.

The more open this chakra, the easier the imagining part of the creative process will be, and the more conscious, and enjoyable.

Our Guardian Angels and Archangel Metatron are wonderful in supporting this part of the manifestation process, if we ask. Our Guardian Presence knows the life plan chosen by our soul and thus, can assist with the ideation/creation most aligned with our mission. Metatron, the Archangel that most helps us with understanding and wisdom, can help us with the process of thinking about our "idea baby," and fleshing out the idea to become clearer. He can help us understand the "why" of the project—why it is important and worthy of our creative juice. We create with our thoughts, so this time is not throwaway time but the foundation of what is to come. The "baby" here begins to take form in the "womb."

Manifestation Example: At this step toward my soul mission, I thought about and saw clearly what form the book could/would take, work done at the level of consciousness and clairvoyance, governed by my third eye, or sixth chakra. Thank you, Angels!

Throat Chakra

The Throat Chakra is all about authenticity and speaking our Truth in the world. This is an important passage in manifestation, as it is where we begin to create with our words! We begin to talk about our "baby" (our idea, our project), and in doing so, more energy of creation gathers around it. The key here is to be discerning about who we decide to share our "baby" with! Will we confide in a critic, someone who hates babies? Or will we find ourselves a cheerleader, a nanny for our "baby"? So important!

A Word about Critics and Cheerleaders

When we have an inspiration, once it is clear to us, the process of manifestation will spontaneously lead us to want to share it, to put words to it, to find a witness for it. This, of course, means that the person to whom we turn to fulfill this role may likely give us their opinion . . . and this, too, is done with words that create!

So we need to watch out at this step. Will we find someone open and supportive (a cheerleader)? Or will we self-sabotage, and turn toward a baby-hating critic? The birth or abortion of our "idea baby" may hang in the balance . . .

Critics

We all have 'em in our lives! Folks who, almost no matter what we have to say, will find the negative in it, the concern, the problem. When we turn to these people, we might think they are honest in their evaluation, but it is very likely that their anything-but-rose-colored glasses taint their appreciation of your beautiful "baby." Such people sometimes are themselves blocked, and do not even realize that their negative comments might be an expression of jealousy, or they simply have difficulty in recognizing anything good in the world. It is important to explore why we would turn to such people in the first place? Are we seeking them out to kill our idea because we are afraid of success? Or afraid of failure?

Whatever the reason, sharing our "idea baby" with a critic is self-sabotaging behavior. In order to give our "idea baby's" birth, or manifestation, a chance, it is a good idea to find a cheerleader/nanny for our idea baby, instead.

Cheerleaders

You might well be, at least some of the time, a cheerleader yourself; most Lightworkers are! A cheerleader is positive and upbeat. They are sufficiently happy in their own lives to want to share your Joy. They are open and appreciative of the creative process, in general, and of the people they care about, specifically (and they find it easy to care about others).

But we are not talking about an empty flatterer here! A cheerleader will honestly give feedback, appreciating the strong points and gently pointing out any gaps in the presentation. The fact that such a person is vibrant reflects on their own happiness and alignment with their sweet spot, and they know, the more the merrier! Cheerleaders are perfect "baby nannies" for your nascent idea!

Think of the people around you. Who are the cheerleaders? Who are the critics? If you had an actual baby, would you let a critic (a nanny who hates babies) babysit? Or would you choose a cheerleader-nanny, someone who loves life and loves babies? In the same way, when you are at this point in the process of manifestation, use your inner discernment, your clairvoyance in whatever form is clear to you, to turn to the people who will be supportive of your process, truly.

Or, if you feel like there are no cheerleaders around you at a given time, talk to your Angels—but stay away from the critics when the project baby is young and tender!

Our Angels and Archangel Sandalphon are excellent cheerleaders for us at this point in the process of creation. Sandalphon, you will recall, is the Archangel of Music, and He can help us sing our metaphorical song in this life by cultivating the speaking around our project that will support its coming to fruition.

Manifestation Example: At this step toward my soul mission, specifically this book, I spoke about my book to two publishers. One who thought (logically, I might add) I needed to become more well known before issuing another book, and another who was eager for my baby. Guess who I decided to collaborate with? Thank you, Angels!

Heart Chakra

The Heart Chakra is our linchpin between Earth and Sky, the connector between our human aspect and our soul. Heart is the blanket fort of our human inner child, which holds the key to our Joy and creation, and it beats in unison with the universal sacred heart.

At this point in the manifestation process, it is time for some soul searching, literally! Knowing that the soul seeded in the child the blueprint for our mission, it is important to spend some time at our heart chakra, the inner compass, or GPS, to feel into whether *all* of you, the entirety of your being, really wants this to happen; whether you are ready; whether it is the right time and the right project; whether the "baby" wants to be born, and if they are ready to be born.

How could it be otherwise? Well, sometimes we might feel that something is an inspiration, when perhaps it is more the ego looking for self-aggrandizement (which is basically the whole purpose of the ego, so this would be normal). Perhaps the project is pure inspiration, but there needs to be maturation before it can come to fruition.

By going within, we can feel into whether there is a joyful desire around the project; whether there is actually an *eek-yay* with regards to it. By doing this, we can save ourselves and others time and energy, concentrating only on birthing babies whose time has come!

Our Angels and Archangel Gabriel(le) are excellent allies to help us with the test below, feeling into the deepest part of our creative self to see if we are wholly on board for this manifestation, and if not, what hesitations might be there. Archangel Gabriel (or Gabrielle if you, like me, like to recognize this feminine energy that is an aspect of Divine Mother) has a wonderful way with inner children and can guide us to the Truth of it.

Let's begin . . .

Exercise
THE HEART CHAKRA/INNER CHILD CHECK-IN

1 Breathing and relaxing, become centered.

2 Set the intention to feel, see, or know whether the child within us is on board with our "baby"; whether there is Joy around the project;whether the timing is right, with not too much *eek* and plenty of *yay*. Ask the Angels to help.

3 Open the channel down to Mother Earth and up to Source. Ask our Guardian Angels and Archangel Gabriel(le) to guide the process with the inner child we are about to undertake.

4 When open, imagine your project, as you see it so far, as a ball of light, shining. The Angels can help you with this; after all, the inspiration traveled to you on your Light beam channel! See or feel or know or imagine that you are holding this nascent creation in your hands. Does it feel sacred? Are you perhaps moved? When you feel it fully, continue.

5 At the level of the heart, imagine your inner child is in front of you, back under the covers, cozily safe in the blanket fort of heart. Call softly to them, saying you have a surprise. When the child, curious, emerges, extend your hands holding the project (perhaps shining?) to the child, saying, "Do you want to play with me and the Angels?" Watch or feel or sense the reaction; whether there is delight or fear, excitement or boredom, or something else. Let the child hold the project in their hands, if they willingly take it. Remain with it until you are clear.

6 Gratitude! Thank your Angels, Archangel Gabrielle, Mother Earth, the child, and yourself. This was good work/play. All the best work is!

Coming back fully, it will likely be clear if you are meant to proceed with the project (that is, if it is aligned with your soul mission) or not. The level of Joy and not too much fear (the old *eek-yay* will be a key). If the child hesitated, seek out and address the concerns that are there. It may be that you might just need to take it slowly. In all creation/manifestation, it is a good idea to proceed at the speed that is comfortable for the slowest part of our being, not the Speedy Gonzales bits!

If necessary, ask the Angels and Archangel Gabrielle to help you reassure that most tender creative part of yourself before continuing.

Manifestation Example: At this step toward the part of my soul mission, which is writing this book, I needed to do a check-in, because the first publisher's hesitation made me doubt myself. When I checked in, I saw the child grab the Light that became a shining book, open it, and clap her hands in utter excitement. I felt that Joy within me, dissolving the crustiness that was the hesitation, recognizing that logic plays little part on my path. Thank you, Angels!

Solar Plexus Chakra

The Solar Plexus Chakra is the seat of our power and our capacity to be confident and stand in our power in the world. If the Heart Chakra exercise has confirmed that you are happily committed to the project, here is where there will be another outreach into the world; a tiny step toward the culmination of your project is in order.

When we take a step, even a tiny one, in the direction of our dreams, the Universe takes note and moves with us. "As our attention goes, so goes the energy," so when we ground it with a tangible step, an action, it calls forth the responding creative energy of the Universe! This is not dissimilar to what happens when a human baby takes their first steps: the adults that witness it rush forward in support and delight!

Here, we apply the important points for successful manifesting, beginning with an action that is easy, fun, specific, able to be achieved without outside help, and meets the *eek-yay* balance standard; that is, it is more exciting than scary.

For the individual plans we will be creating in the next chapter, we will need to ensure that each step of the plan meets those criteria in order to ensure the success of our aligning to mission.

Our Angels and Archangel Michael are excellent allies to help us step into our power with the contemplated action. Archangel Michael is the Power of God, and we, as God's creation, are looking to express that power in our creation. He can help and guide us in this.

Manifestation Example: Stepping into my power in the manifestation process of this book was the actual writing of the table of contents and the book proposal to send to the chosen publisher. This showed the universe I was serious . . . and it showed me, too! Thank you, Angels!

Sacral Chakra

The Sacral Chakra is the seat of our creativity, sensuality, and sexuality. This step in the manifestation process invites us to express our creativity. It is time to set our inner child free, releasing the natural creativity with which we were born. It is time to let the "idea/project baby" grow!

The fact that this chakra also relates to our sexuality and sensuality is not an accident. The more we are living wholly in our body, the more we appreciate our physical being, the more what we manifest in the physical world is supported ("Energy seeks equilibrium"). Thus, if someone is not comfortable in their body, or rejects any aspect of it, it is a good idea to address that imbalance in order to create. Even something simple like receiving a massage, or rubbing our own hands or feet with cream, can be a boon to creativity!

Our Angels and Archangel Jophiel are excellent allies to help us with the movement of creation, as Jophiel is (as we know) the Beauty of God, who will ensure the beauty of our creation (if we ask for and accept Her aid). Technical point: Of course, when we call on Angels to assist, we do not need to define which step they are to help us with, thus, Jophiel can help all the way through, as the whole process is a creation. She will help us maintain a High energy around our project by keeping our thoughts, words, and emotions of High frequency, positive, thereby cultivating a shining confidence in our field that will attract only the Highest and best.

When we are consciously accompanied by the Angels, our creation becomes co-creation! Of course, pure inspiration is always a co-creation. Knowing this and welcoming it consciously will fortify the help that is there for us along our path.

Manifestation Example: This step of my mission expression of writing this book was, well, writing this book. What I am up to right now—accompanied by the Angels, of course, and connected to the child within me and the soul who is the Truth of me. Gratitude! Thank you, Angels!

Root Chakra

The Root Chakra is the energetic seat of our human existence, governing the material aspect of our being: health, home, work, and money. We spoke earlier of how when we take a step forward, the Universe responds.

Well, when we launch our creativity, the Universe works with us, moving us in a Flow toward the elements needed to birth our "baby." Even if the creation process seems solitary, the birthing invites the world to participate.

Our Angels and Archangel Raphael are excellent allies as we look toward this birth. In addition to human collaborators, our Angels are always at the ready to whisper in our hearts words of encouragement and helpful guidance. Raphael is the Archangel of Divine Healing, which always brings us into alignment with heavenly Truth; as such, He ensures that the manifestation of our inspired project attracts the right energies to align with the project energetically, as the project already exists in the eternal ("As above, so below!"). Who better than a Divine healer to welcome a baby with heavenly genes into the world?

Manifestation Example: The final step of this particular manifestation, this book, has already occurred in the French version, and now, the English "baby" is on its way to being born. Once I took the step of writing, allies emerged to continue the birthing here in the material plane: editors, publishers, marketing and PR folks, and the media. The impact of this birthing is already underway! The heavens have guided me to partnerships for this "baby," some tried and true and some new, and the team is magic. As a result, there is a little eek in me, but oh so much yay! Thank you, Angels!

In the next chapter, we will use everything we have done so far to put together a mission statement and a plan for the next 12 months to tangibly shift us into high-gear alignment, Re-membering soul and our mission!

Chapter 12
SOUL PLAN AND
MISSION STATEMENT

*W*e have done the good work of preparing, and likely at this point we can agree that your overall mission is probably that of a Lightworker. That said, we can't all have the same mission, can we?

Well, yes and no.

Yes, because we are each and every one of us expressing Source or God energy here on Earth in this lifetime. And people who are Lightworkers, specifically, have all been of service since the beginning of living here on Earth, even while unconscious of having such a plan or mission. But, no, of course not! Each one of us is unique, and our very being-ness, our instruments were specifically designed to play the Game of Life to optimize our chance of aligning to the plan (which we had forgotten but might be Re-membering) of our soul, our mission.

Since being born into life on Earth brought us, by necessity, through The Forgetting, most of us may have also experienced the burial of the blueprint of our plan, as it became hidden under layers of "gunk" (worry, stress, and fear, as well as limiting beliefs about how one "should" live and what our capabilities are).

In the work we have already done with our inner child, who our friends are, who we admire and whose journey we wish we could emulate, and our secret dreams, we have already dug up the most salient elements of our plan, uncovering the basis of our personal soul mission. The groundwork has been laid when we recognize that the child we were was closer to the blueprint than we are as adults, and we have already cut through the "gunk" covering the most important highlights.

We also have done the work to recognize that what was planted in us is always in our energetic field, attracting people who are called in similar directions (or have had similar trauma)—friends and acquaintances, or even people we don't know, who we admire greatly. We may even be drawn mores strongly to notice them, to the point that jealousy might express itself with regard to the specific aspects of their journey!

We have recognized the obstacles that might be blocking us and their solutions, and have seen how manifestation works in theory. Time to put it into practice!

We have done some good detective work already and identified a list of personal values. However, the idea of this book is not only to recognize those elements that are important to our soul mission but also to align our human life purpose to it! For that, we will need a plan.

The Plan

The idea here is to create a human plan to turn our boats around in order to align with the route proposed by soul, the mission for our life.

Why is this goal worthy of our time? There are many reasons, but the most important are more Joy and less regret:

1 Creating and following this plan will bring us into our sweet spot of soul alignment, so we will have *more Joy*.
2 This plan, when followed, will bring us into alignment with our mission, so that we feel *less regret* in our daily lives, and also at the very end of our Game here on Earth.

Before we get into the nitty-gritty of forming a plan, let's surround ourselves with the help that is there for us, shall we?

The "outer" experts—our Angels and the "inner" experts, our soul and inner child—are ready and willing and, in fact, are waiting to accompany us in this. Ironically, though our guides and Angels are "outer" experts, we may feel their presence and connect with them from deep within. Together with our "inner" experts (our sacred Soul and innocence of the inner child), they form a team which supports our game of life wholly and powerfully as we find our way to fulfill our mission

We'll begin, then, by opening our channels to them before moving into the creation of the plan together!

 Exercise

ENERGETIC PREPARATION BEFORE CREATING THE PLAN

1 Breathe

Focus on your breath, remembering that Life is carried on the breath. Breathe in the life that awaits you, breathe out the life that came before.

2 Set your intention

Remember that the most important part of any energetic protocol is the intention you bring to it. Set your intention to call in the Heavens (your Angels and soul) and Earth (your human inner child and Mother Earth, Gaia) so you can create your plan with the help and support of the whole team. We will be inviting Archangel Michael, head of the Lightworkers Union, to support your finding of the path Highest for you at this time.

3 Open the channel down to the earth

Use your now-open channel to anchor (ground) yourself, following your Light down to the heart of the planet to be supported in your task of creating your plan for earthly manifestation of soul mission. A simple phrase from the heart will suffice, such as:

Dear Mother, thank you in advance for your support of my manifestation, bringing more Joy to the planet, an expression of my Love for you.

Arriving at the center, seeing Mother Earth/Gaia is waiting for you with open arms, allow her to hold you now, and throughout the planning process. Use your channel to return to the body, heart full.

4 Open the channel up to the Heavens

From your heart, follow your Light to the Heavens, uplifted, carried on the wings of your Angels, the Guardian Presence, returning to Source, where your soul ever lives. In that space, call on soul (who chose the child) to help the reconnection, with words of your own, perhaps something like this:

Greetings, dear soul. Today is planning day! I ask your clear guidance in this important work, so I might follow more easily the trail of clues you have gifted me. Guide me in planning my steps to align with you, and with our mission. Thank you!

While in the Source space, it is a good time to formally call on our Guardian Angels as well, perhaps something like this:

Loving Angels, I gratefully accept your guidance and Love as I create my soul plan, just as we planned even before I was born! Thank you!

Lastly, while here, it would be a good idea to call on Archangel Michael to help us find our Highest path as Lightworkers:

Archangel Michael, you who express the pure Power of the Love of God, protect and guide me on my path, helping me to create the next steps to standing in my power, in the Light and Love of my shining soul mission. Thank you!

With each invitation, take a moment and feel or see or know that there is a response to your prayer.

When you are ready, with your soul and the Angels accompanying you, allow yourself to fully Flow back down into your body to the level of your heart, the home of the inner child.

5 Calling for the child

At the heart, imagine or see or feel that lovely child under the covers again, in front of you but maybe already peeking out, just waiting for your invitation. In your own words, invite the child along for the planning session, perhaps saying:

Our time is here, dear one, and I cannot do our best job without you! Please join us—me and our soul, the Angels, and Archangel Michael— to make our plan. Bring your ebullience and creativity, your enthusiasm and Light, your Joy and honesty, so we can step fully and play our Game joyfully together now!

You may see the child jump up and run to you, or simply hear or know their yes! A whispered thank you, and off we go.

6 Gratitude sealing the deal

Place your hands on your heart to seal the deal with your soul plan team: Angels and Archangel Michael, you, your soul, and your inner child. They are exactly what is needed for human and soul and Angelic manifestation! Stay in that powerful, creative space until you feel complete and ready!

Let's Go! Creating the Plan

We will work together to create a plan for the next 12 months; going farther out doesn't make any sense, as the first 12 months will already shift our energy sufficiently to change us, opening up to new possibilities. It is always a good idea to review/redo the plan every year or so, especially if we have followed it, and so, are ready for our next steps! I will continue to show my work here, with the goal of rendering the process very clear. Finally, in the process described below, we will call on Angelic assistance. As always, this is optional, as we can find our soul path on our own; however, why not render this easier with the help that is available to us?

Planning Process

Find the list of values you created (mine is on page 115) after the Inner Child questions. As a reminder, this list represents things that were important to you (either they provided Joy or they were lacking) as a child.

Now, add any other values that are not already on your original Inner Child list, such as those that came up in the other exercises: Your Questions about Who Your Friends are (mine are musicians, specifically singer/guitarists and poets); The Desire or Dream You Keep Secret (mine is singing); and Those You Admire and Those You Wish You Could Emulate (mine were guitarist and spiritually powerful singer John Denver; nature-as-muse poet Mary Oliver; and actress and fluent French speaker Jodie Foster).

When you have added your "friends, dream and admiration/envy" values, rank them, too, in order of the importance you feel when you think of them. This is not the time to analyze what is most logical, or most achievable in the world's terms, but what you FEEL is most important to you, as expressed through your instrument, your body. What is your heart telling you? Take some time to listen . . . why not ask your Guardian Angels to help?

Kathryn's Answers

Here is my list, incorporating those last elements:

1 Spirituality
2 Human Love and Affection, Family and Friends
3 Peace and Quiet (rare at home or elsewhere, library)
4 Sports, Exercise
5 Nature, Water
6 Music (guitar and singing)
7 Poetry
8 Healthy Eating
9 Languages, Travel
10 Books (reading and writing)
11 Acting
12 Having a Mentor (teacher, coach)
13 Money
14 Freedom
15 Safety/Protection

Next, using your list, create a subset list we will call Things that Are Not Yet Manifest; that is, those things that you do not experience as very active in your life today. Choose items that you don't already have much of in your life, and not things that you already express in life well. (For example, my life is focused more on the spiritual than anything else, and I have a great deal of silence and peace in my life, so though these are high on my value scale, I won't include them on my list.)

Instead, focus on highly-placed values that you do not yet experience much or even at all. Intentionally introducing new (valued) experience into our lives shifts our whole energy field and allows us to align with our highest and best, attracting what is optimal for us, allowing the road to rise to meet us instead of chasing after it.

So what will you choose that is Not Yet Manifest for you?

Kathryn's List of Values of Things That Are Not Yet Manifest

1 Family and Friends

Because of where and how I live, much of my contact with family and friends is at a distance, and virtual.

2 Nature and Water

Living in Paris, a big city, currently there is not enough contact with the wild, with the natural world, in my everyday life.

3 Music (Guitar and Singing)

I would like to learn guitar and sing more, even if only for my own amusement, at home.

4 Poetry

I have always enjoyed both reading and writing poetry, but haven't been doing much of either lately.

5 Acting

I have enjoyed performing in improv groups and short films in the past, but have not been doing much of this at all of late, focused on other forms of creative expression.

Once you have a good list, choose **three** of the "sweet spot" experiences you long to express (and recognize as important to your soul and mission) and incorporate into your Soul Alignment plan for the next 12 months and also to, literally, "in-corp-orate"; that is, *make them part of your body and part of your daily experience.*

Here, if it makes sense, you can combine some of the elements into one grouping. For example, if you have Nature and Horseback Riding on your list as two separate elements, you can combine them.

For each element on the last list, we can see that they would be great to add into our lives, but we already have noted ***the importance of not setting the bar too high*** as well as the importance of setting a goal ***we can achieve*** *on our own power* (without the help of others) in order to ensure success, right? So here, choose 3 maximum, and only those you can do on your own. Here are mine:

Kathryn's Top Three Values, and Why

Of the five values not expressed in my life, as much as I would like to keep them at this time, two are going to be excluded from my plan at the outset, since they contradict one of the five important points for human manifestation we saw earlier, but which bear repeating here:

All steps should be:

1 **exciting, but not scary** (the *eek-yay* standard)
2 **clear and concise** as to "what" and "when," and thus, actionable
3 **easy to achieve!**
4 **possible to undertake on our own** (not dependent on someone else)
5 **fun!**

Eliminations from Kathryn's List

From my previous list, I am going to opt not to include Friends and Family and Acting on this new list, because most of the steps that cultivate this value would **require the involvement of others.** So here is my list of three values to incorporate in my Soul Plan for the next 12 months:

1 Nature and Water

Living in a big city like Paris, there is not enough opportunity for contact with the wild, natural world, in my everyday life.

2 Music (Guitar and Singing)

I would like to learn guitar and sing more, even if only for my own amusement, at home.

3 Poetry
I have always enjoyed both reading and writing poetry but haven't been doing much of either lately.

Once you have your (maximum) three values you want to incorporate, create a chart, something like this:

Value	3 Months	6 Months	12 Months
Nature			
Music			
Poetry			

Then, begin to fill in each box. What small, easy step will you take toward that sweet-spot soul value: in the next three months? In the next six months? In the coming year?

Think of each empty box in your chart as an Invitation: from life, from the Angels, from your Soul, from your inner child: an invitation to stretching and growing, to mystery and adventure, to exploring experiences for which your heart yearns. Desires which have lain hidden, or simply those for which you have not given yourself permission to explore. Each one of these values are very important to your joy and thus to your light shining, to your life purpose!

Take your time. Get quiet and hear what your heart is saying. Feel what the inner child is saying? Does it meet those five criteria for successful manifestation?

1 *Is it exciting but not scary* (the *eek-yay* standard)?
2 *Is it clear and concise as to "what" and "when," and so, actionable?*
3 *Is it easy to achieve* (baby steps!)?
4 *Is it possible to undertake on our own* (not dependent on someone else)?
5 *Is it fun?*

On the next page you'll find an example, mine, to make things even clearer.

Kathryn's Soul Plan

Value	3 Months	6 Months	12 Months
Nature	Visit the River Seine once a week for at least 5 minutes when in Paris.	Visit Parc de St. Cloud at least once, and connect with the fairies.	Visit Emerald Isle, North Carolina, the pelicans, and the dolphins one time.
Music	Sing a song, any song, every day.	Learn the basic guitar chords.	Play a Beatles song.
Poetry	Read Mary Oliver once a week.	Write a poem.	Publish a poem online.

Let's further discuss my "baby" steps in light of the five criteria to get more clarity. We will use my first value, **Nature,** to develop this further.

Nature

Three Months:
Visit the River Seine once a week for at least 5 minutes

1 *Exciting but not scary (the* eek-yay *standard)?* Yes! I often do not take the time to be in Nature. This would be great!
2 *Clear and concise as to "what" and "when", and so, actionable?* Yes!
3 *Easy to achieve (baby steps!!!)?* Yes. The Seine is not far from where I live.
4 *Possible to undertake on our own (not dependent on someone else)?* Yes.
5 *Fun?* Yes!

Six Months:
Visit Parc de St. Cloud at least once, and connect with the fairies

1 *Exciting but not scary (the* eek-yay *standard)?* Yes. I almost never go there, so this would be a great way to get my fresh air and Nature, and time for ME!
2 *Clear and concise as to "what" and "when", and thus, actionable?* Yes. I teach connecting with fairies and elementals, so this is doable.

3 *Easy to achieve (baby steps!!!)?* Yes. The park is not far from where I live, a short bus ride, or a long walk.

4 *Possible to undertake on our own (not dependent on someone else)?* Yes.

5 *Fun?* Yes!

12 Months:
Visit Emerald Isle, North Carolina, the pelicans and the dolphins once

1 *Exciting but not scary (the* eek-yay *standard)?* YES . . . I dream of this place almost every day!

2 *Clear and concise as to "what" and "when", and so, actionable?* Yes. Within the coming year, I plan to go home to the US at least once, so this is very doable.

3 *Easy to achieve (baby steps!)?* Yes—as above.

4 *Possible to undertake on our own (not dependent on someone else)?* Yes.

5 *Fun?* Yes!

For each value/sweet spot that you have targeted for incorporating into your life, do the same exercise until you have your plan complete, and are happy with it.

EXAMPLE: A Word about the Plan

It should be noted that the plan you create here is not the soul's plan (which is the End Game), but your plan, the human plan, an intermediary step. Sure, it is influenced by soul, and supported by Angels, but the 12-month plan you have created will shake things up energetically and align you with your sweet spots, and thus, with your soul.

The fact that the soul plan I just created includes music does not mean that I am destined to be a musician, but that music will be important on my path to fulfilling why I was born, what my soul mission is.

I recognize already that this is so: Without knowing what will be shaken up further, I already receive messages from the

Angels through music lyrics, and I am delighted (lit up!) when singing along or listening to live music.

I have sufficient nervousness (a whole lotta eek!) about learning to play the guitar that I know it is important on my path. For me, likely not to be a professional, but more to allow my creativity to express further. Every creative activity amps up our light, and contributes to the Flow of our path, the ease of our alignment and Re-membering.

For example, the very first time I did the admiration/envy exercise, my banker job here in Paris was about to end and I was completely lost. As I alluded to earlier, what came up for me was Jodie Foster (sound familiar), specifically, her quality of acting. So, I went to acting school a week after my job ended, imagining that my soul was telling me to follow my then-secret dream, and become an actress. I was wrong!

In fact, in acting school, one learns to peel away the layers covering our authentic self, our real emotions, and I had a lot of both that had been hidden away! Behind walls, yes, but more like fortresses, complete with moats and crocodiles!

Through my acting studies, I opened up and learned to allow emotions, to be vulnerable, to open up to others, even publicly. That capacity serves me today in my soul work, when I speak to individuals and groups all over the world. The Universe, evidently, sometimes gives us only one step at a time, and that is for the better! If I had known what lay in store for me, I would have run the other way! It is just as well that all of this is on a need-to-know basis!

From the above we see once more that the 12-month plan (which led me to acting school back then) is not in itself the soul mission, but a vital and revitalizing step toward that perfect alignment. So why not . . .

Will you play?

Creating this plan in itself will not get you out from under your blanket fort and out of bed, though. In order to bring your light out from under the covers, it will be necessary to play with your plan! Will you play? One step at a time, every day, first for one month, then for three, then for the last six making up the year, will you . . . ?

Commit!

Hand on heart, commit to yourself, your inner child, your soul, your Angels, Mother Earth, and Archangel Michael to execute the plan in the months to come. As ever, do this in your own words, but it could be something like:

> *I, (insert name here), commit this day to executing the plan we have come up with faithfully in order to align with my Soul and mission, with my childlike Joy and creativity, with the powerful support of Mother Earth, and the guidance and protection of the Angels and Archangels, especially Michael. Great gratitude!*

It is always interesting to write this out, perhaps right under where you have written the plan, or even create and decorate a Plan and Engagement suitable for framing, so you can look at it every day for the coming year, knowing that you are up to sacred work!

Mission Statement of a Lightworker

Why would a Lightworker need a Mission Statement?

To REMEMBER—and stay Re-membered! A Mission Statement is meant to remind us that we are lightworkers and that our mission here is important. This is not a small thing! The world in its madness makes us forget our Selves, our light; the Mission Statement is meant to help us remember it, to stay focused on it, so we can maintain our commitment to it, and to our joy, our peace.

Before we complete here, let's create the mission statement that can go along with that engagement. We will need to create two lists.

First, make a list of things you love (or would love) to do. You can use activities from the previous lists, if you like, as long as you come up with 10 activities to start off with.

EXAMPLE:
Kathryn's List of Things She Loves to Do

(In no special order, as they come to mind, knowing my channel is still open):

1 Playing
2 Writing
3 Singing
4 Hiking
5 Swimming
6 Loving
7 Teaching
8 Energy Work
9 Making People Laugh
10 Playing Music

Now, imagine the world as you wish it were. List of up to three aspects of that wonderful world that would be present if you had your druthers.

EXAMPLE:
Kathryn's List of Aspects of Her Perfect World

(Again, listed in no special order, as they come to mind, knowing my channel is still open):

1 Peace on Earth
2 Love between Humans and All Beings
3 Music

Now, choose the three most loved items from your first list, things you love (or would love) to do.

EXAMPLE:
Kathryn's Sub-List of Three Things She Loves to Do

(Again, in no special order, as they come to mind, knowing my channel is still open):

1 Playing
2 Writing
3 Teaching

Now, insert your lists into this sentence:

"I, (insert name), Lightworker, express the shining of my mission by (insert activity no. 1 here), (insert activity no. 2 here), and (insert activity no. 3 here) to create a world of peace, love, and music.

EXAMPLE:
Kathryn's Mission Statement as of Today

"I, Kathryn Hudson, Lightworker, express my shining of my mission by playing, writing, and teaching to create a world of peace, love, and music."

Now, well prepared with a Soul Plan and Mission statement, The Forgetting has been Re-membered. Time for the second part of the Game!

Afterword

RELAX AND ENJOY—
FOR A STRONG FINISH!

*P*hew! That was a lot of work. Bravo! Hopefully it was also fun! (the fifth criterion for success in human manifestation but definitely not the least important! Joy aligns us directly to soul!).

Once you have set the plan in motion, relax! Once you have done the work, take a breather. Of course, stay up to date with the soul plan you created, but you created it to be easy for a reason!

The most important part of the soul plan we create is not our activity (though every step signals to the universe that we are clear-intentioned, inviting the collaboration of Angels), but our very powerful *intention*.

As children of creator, we create. When we do so intentionally, consciously, it is much more powerful than all the unconscious creation that we may have manifested before. This life that we are living truly becomes like a game: joyful and fluid, where we Re-member Who We Are, Truly (an eternal soul), so we sweat the details less.

While it can be interesting to go through the 12-month Soul Plan process again annually to ensure that we stay in that juicy sweet spot, well beyond our initial plan, it is most important to remain aware, present, and conscious in our oh-so-creative thoughts! But there are some tricks of the manifestation trade that are helpful to know, so let's look at them in this final chapter.

Clear Intentions

While using our own language and words that come from the heart is generally the most powerful way to manifest, there are a few guidelines that may prove helpful. In setting intentions, it is interesting to avoid words like "want" or "wish," because the Universe is more a mirror than an interpreter, reflecting back to us what we are emanating rather than taking orders, interpreting them, and filling them.

Let's take a look.

Imagine we say "I want to be thinner/healthier/happier!" Since the Universe reflects back to us what we emanate, what we put forth, we can imagine the Universal response: "You want to be thinner, healthier, happier!"

Instead of using such phrases (which confirm that we are lacking something), the idea is to set intentions that focus on the fulfillment we are looking for: "I intend to enjoy good health, happiness, fitness," or even, going farther and stronger, "I enjoy fitness, happiness, and health."

Love Where You Are

In addition to clear intention, another key to conscious (co-)creation going forward is to remain in the sweet spot that your 12-month plan is designed to create, getting you consciously into the Flow, your vessel moving naturally in alignment and mission fruition.

But before we are living and loving in the sweet spot, it will help us to love where we are, right now! At any point, if we reject what is happening, if we resist either where we are or who we are with or what we are doing, we fill our energetic field with resistance that will block our Highest from Flowing to us.

This does not mean that we lie to ourselves. If we are not happy with any aspect of our life, of course we should take steps and set intention to change it, but NOT complain about it, NOT gripe about it, NOT lament about it! Especially if we want something to change, we need to ensure that our energetic field is filled with positive proactive (not negative or reactive) energy.

Specifically, we need to get rid of language like "I never have any luck" and replace it instead with "In the past, I didn't have much luck, but now I am shifting and playing the Game in abundance!" In addition to the words, if you can use your intention and imagination to *feel* what that abundance feels like, you are already welcoming it and attracting it to you!

That positive energy expresses Life, Love, and the Power of creation, and as we know, "Energy seeks equilibrium" and "Like attracts like!"

Inner GPS (Heart)

Once we let go of our blanket forts/comfort zone, and also let go of resistance, the Flow picks up and things become even more interesting. New people, places, and opportunities come Flowing toward us, as opposed to us chasing them down, like the world teaches is necessary to do, as long as we are willing to step through the doors that open for us.

So the question is: How willing are you for things to change?

If you are willing, as the Flow picks up, it is a good idea to keep a firm hand on the rudder, steering with the help of your inner compass or GPS: your heart. I am speaking here not only about the physical heart, which, by its rate of beating, can give us good information about where to go, but also about the energetic heart, which allows us to feel into what is just and right and good and delightful, and what is not. Our GPS can express every variation and is there to help us, if only we pay attention!

Get into the habit of checking in with your heart whenever you are facing a choice. Ask your Angels (and why not also Archangel Gabrielle?) to facilitate your communication with your vessel, your instrument, your heart. Subtle as it is at first, when you are clear in this intention, and willing to take the time to slow down and get very quiet, you will feel (or see or hear or simply know) which path is the correct one to take and most aligned with your Highest good.

This achieves two things: It clears the haze from the "what next?" mind, leading to clarity, and cultivates our clairvoyant gifts so this practice and others become easier.

Keep It Simple, Sweetie (Relax and Enjoy)

When we recognize that we actually create with our consciousness, it is, of course, empowering (once we no longer find it daunting), but in this book I have also made clear that we don't have to do all of this alone. This helps with the whole "daunting" thing!

As we learn to create and Flow with and toward our highest expression, we will have more and more experiences (you might have these already) that show us we are not alone, and instead, supported, guided, and helped.

When this becomes obvious, something in us begins to relax—the part of us that learned that we have to be always on guard, always defensive and needing to control things.

What a relief! The breath in its fullness comes back, and Life with it. Daily life becomes a treasure hunt. *What delicious thing will happen to remind me that the Angels are here for me today?* Waiting for it, anticipating it, knowing it will come changes everything, and is almost as delightful as seeing that sign or hearing that message.

We all know that we create with our thoughts and words, so now we know to watch ourselves to avoid the pitfall of negativity and negative creation. But can we go even farther?

Yes, and it is simpler!

Imagine that the life waiting for you is even more than you can even imagine (I know that this was the case for me); that your thoughts, however positive, put restrictions on it. We start to play in the playground of "This is pretty good," which is already, well, pretty good, right?

But what if we are meant to be playing in the playground of "amazing!", but we have settled for the garden of "pretty good", simply because we didn't think, didn't know, that better was possible?

The Western world most often teaches us to limit our expectations about life so as to avoid being hurt. But isn't settling for less also hurting us, limiting us? By extension, when we settle for less, we nourish the energetic already too present in the world: settling for less, settling for "pretty good" or even "not bad," both for ourselves and for others.

You know how hard it is to buck the system established around you, *non?* Similarly, breaking the habit of settling for less can seem difficult, but it is well worth it!

If we can do this, releasing the habit of giving ourselves a glass ceiling, the Angels around us, and the whole Universe, will conspire to surprise and delight us, moving us into astonishing synchronicities, helping us Re-member!

This does not mean there won't be challenges; there will, as long as we are alive on Earth. But those challenges will be easier to handle, and we will be graced with the ability to see the blessing behind a challenging situation, even as it arises, making it easier for us to go with the Flow, knowing that all is well, always.

While we might seize the steering wheel of our vehicle once we understand how manifestation works and we know the broad lines of our purpose, perhaps the most interesting and helpful hint of all is to LET GO, to decide that we will not limit our own Game, but will open it up by relaxing.

Can we do that? Isn't it time to step into our power in a way that doesn't limit us? To move, instead, into the simplest solution: collaborative manifestation, with the Universe proposing through Angelic assistance and us saying, "Yes, please" and "Thank you!"

Can we hear, finally, what Love, or Source, has been saying all along: "Don't worry. I've got you!"?

Of course, relaxing is easier if we can transform that pesky fear of death thing . . .

Dying Is Part of Living

This last section speaks to "That Which Shall Not Be Named": Death.

In the Western world, we have a superstitious way of treating dying, something that many cultures deem perfectly natural. In some cultures, the whole family will gather around Grandfather as he makes his transition, and one of the many grandchildren might even see his soul leave the body, perhaps smiling kindly and waving at the child.

Since children in such contexts often remain open longer, seeing Granddad off in this way will appear normal, but whether we clairvoyantly see the person passing or not, accompanying someone who is transitioning in this way reassures people, even from childhood, that death is both normal (nothing to fear), and, in fact, not the end at all.

In a world heavy with fear and the hatred it breeds, transforming fear of death can be a way through, a source of transformation.

In the West, we have robbed ourselves of such social and familial experiences of accompanying loved ones at the moment of their passing, so much so that, far from being a support for the dying person, we sometimes even add stress to their passing, as they try to avoid upsetting us further. Many dying people wait until a loved one has left the room to take their last breath, in the limiting belief that having the loved one there would burden them; knowing that their loved one is holding on and not letting them go adds sadness and stress to the experience of dying.

We keep children from sickness and death, and even many adults can't stand to go to hospital or a funeral. Instead of being a celebration of the person's life, these become terrible events that create lasting trauma, all because people are not taught to look ahead with clarity and have experiences of peaceful passing from a young age. As pertains to our soul mission, many people are so afraid of dying they never get around to living, certainly not the (sometimes audacious) rich life proposed by aligning with soul.

As we look at our soul mission, and begin to recognize its importance to our soul, we open to the Truth that Life continues, indefinitely, after death. The more we work from a soul-level perspective, the more we as humans can get comfortable with that idea, comfortable enough to plan for it, even accompanying ourselves in preparation.

Why is it important to get used to death before it even happens?

Simply put, energetically, *how we leave this life is as important as how we live.* Since we know that no energy is lost (law of conservation of energy), imagine the stress and fear that often accompanies a person's dying, and how that fear weighs on the earth, even after the person's soul has moved on to Higher planes. But when we can get comfortable with the idea of departing peacefully before we are at Death's threshold, we can ensure that we do not contribute to that heavy pall of fear, and even transmute it, thus lessening the density of fear that pervades our world. This is true Lightworker work!

It is easier to befriend death if we already feel our life has mattered, of course, and all the work we have done in this book leads us to fulfilling that objective. In using the exercises proposed in this last section, we can span the veil between this human life and our soul, and use it to easily cross the rainbow bridge (which is not just for animals) peacefully, when the time comes, making our passing easier for those we love.

In the following exercise, we will call on our soul and the Angels, especially Archangel Azrael (the Angel of Death) to help us get used to the idea of death; that is, to reaching beyond this life to touch Life Eternal, thereby ending the limiting and false belief that death is final. This exercise is designed to let us into the secret that death is more a graduation than anything else, something to be celebrated even if humanly we will miss someone (unless we cultivate our clairvoyance).

When we use a bridging exercise like this (and such exercises exist in many modalities and cultures), the fear of death is eased and the fun of life takes on a new lightness.

Sound good? Let's do it!

Exercise

ENERGETIC BRIDGE
TO TRANSFORM THE FEAR OF DEATH

(**Note:** This does not entail an actual near-death experience (NDE), but rather, brings us into calm contemplation of the transition.)

1 Breathe

Focus on your breath, remembering that life is carried on the breath. Breathe in the Life that awaits you; breathe out the life that came before. Recognize that part of the Life that awaits you is that part of Life called Death, that transition.

Breathe in the Life that comes afterward; breathe out the life that is in the past.

2 Set Your Intention

Knowing that intention is the most powerful part of energy work, set your intention to call in the Heavens (your Angels and your soul), as well as the earth (your physical body expression of Mother Earth, or Gaia), in order to span the Bridge and touch and taste the eternal aspect of your Life. We will be inviting Archangel Azrael, Angel of Death and Guardian of the Veil, to support your experience, coming and going for a brief visit at this time.

3 Open the Channel down to the Earth

Ground yourself using your wide-open channel, following your Light to the beating heart of the earth for support in your intention of transforming the fear of death, which weighs heavily on the earth at this time. Use your own words; perhaps something like.

> *Dear Mother, thank you in advance for your support. I would rid myself of this fear, and in so doing, ease the fear that holds all my fellow humans back from living their Highest purpose joyfully. I know this good work will serve to lighten your load.*

Arriving at the center, see that Mother Earth/Gaia is waiting for you and quickly takes you to her heart and fills you with ease of being, so you can approach this experience with curiosity and playfulness. When you feel calm and happy, return, and place your hands and your attention (and thus, your energy) on your heart and continue.

4 Opening the Channel up to the Heavens

Decide to use your channel now, and from your heart, follow your Light up to the Heavens, accompanied by Angel wings. Arriving at Source, where your soul lives eternally, take the time to Re-member the soul that (with God or Source) chose you and is you: the Truth of you, and eternal. Call on soul to help you release the fear of death, perhaps with words something like this:

> *My dear soul, thank you. We are growing closer and closer, and my life is the richer for it. But I am still plagued by the limiting beliefs of humanity at this time. Please help me release the fear of dying. Even though I know intellectually that nothing ends, help me feel it in my body, help me breathe it and live it and release all blocks to it now, so that, thus freed, I can live fully the mission you have chosen for us. Thank you!*

At this time, call on the Guardian Angels also, and build a team to accompany you in this work, perhaps with something like:

> *Loving Angels, help me release that which does not serve: the fear of death that infringes upon my soul Joy and the power of my path. Remind me, please, that before "me" and after "me," we play in the Garden. Thank you!*

Lastly, while here, it is a great idea to call on Archangel Azrael to help us see death clearly as a doorway to God, so that fear falls away:

> *Archangel Azrael, you who bring comfort to the dying and the dead, great bright Light of Transition, help me now to calm the fear of that passage in advance so I might be a font of hope and transformation for the rest of my days shining. Thank you!*

With each invitation, take a moment and feel or see or know that there is a response to your prayer.

When you are ready, with your soul and the Angels accompanying you, allow yourself to Flow back down fully into your body to the level of your heart, where your heart beats in unison with the sacred heart of the Universe.

5 Slowing the Body

At the heart, imagine or see or feel a lovely blanket fort that beckons to you, a peaceful space of safety, where all is well and there is rest to be had.

Life has been busy and noisy, and a respite is so attractive, to leave the business of life, even for just a while. Climb under the covers. There, you find the child, delighted that this time you have come for them, instead of always drawing them into the fray with you. Now the child shows you, in all innocence and purity, that there is nothing to fear here.

Your eyes close, and the blanket covering you allows you to hide far from the world and its form of life. The blanket space muffles the noisy world to stillness. All there is here and now is breath.

Breathe in slowly. Allow your breath to slow, nothing forced. As calm settles in, breath slows naturally. Know that soul and Angels and Azrael are near, though in the dark you likely do not see them.

Focus on your body—how still it is, how calm. In this present moment, you are entirely here. Notice the tingling of your fingertips, perhaps, or the sound of your heartbeat. Feel the respite that is here, nothing to worry about, no more battles to wage or problems to solve.

Imagine that your time is done. Now you can watch over those you love, and perhaps send them signs so that they don't fear death, either, so they can fully live!

Remain with the Angels and Archangel Azrael at your eternal soul level, which will look after your loved ones, cocooned with the child within you, perfectly safe and comfortable under the soft covers of the blanket fort/veil. Stay in the blanket fort until you feel like it is complete for you. Return as often as you feel called to do so; with every visit, the veil thins, and the peace of an eternal perspective replaces fear.

6 Gratitude Sealing the Deal

Place your hands on your heart to seal the deal with your Soul Plan team: Angels and Archangel Azrael, your soul and your inner child—exactly what is needed for Divine Re-membering! Stay in that powerful gratitude until you feel solid and strong, standing in your power, ready for your mission!

Before we close out our time together, just a word about what happens AFTER the mission, if you are curious?

Judgment Day or Divine Debrief?

One last item to discuss before we leave the subject of finishing strong is what happens right after we die. As we discussed in the first part of this book, Archangel Azrael accompanies us when we pass, the brilliant white Light that we have heard about so often from people who have died and come back. But what then?

If you grew up as I did, there may be (mixed up with other fears of dying) a "thing": a fear of judgment, of fire and brimstone. The Angels want us to know that that "thing" is not a thing. Judgment exists only here on Earth, in the duality of this plane. Humans judge; God integrates.

That is not to say that nothing happens after we die. There is a moment of debriefing with Archangel Jeremiel, who is, after all, the *misericordia* of God, Mercy! The debrief is not about judging the human for what happened on Earth, as the human aspect of us that went through The Forgetting and has Now Re-membered is gone, and we are just soul; rather, it is a check-in about our soul mission. Was it a success? If so, what will our next evolutionary step/mission be (or will there be another one?). If the mission was not achieved, knowing what went wrong and what went right will refine the plan for the next lifetime.

If the life that just ended was heavy and difficult, there is a restorative session (imagine a heavenly spa!) that will go a long way to erasing all trace of hardship, save that which is karmic. The imprint of all karmic imbalance will be carried into the next lifetime, with soul and Source choosing the role, the human life, that will optimize the possibility of balancing karma.

We complete here with gratitude—for the Angels, the Archangels, the children within us, our souls, and ourselves! Every time one of us Re-members, the Earth reaps the benefit of that Light and Love, that peace and transformation.

Go, Lightworkers, go! Mission Fruition!

My Soul Plan Chart

*I*nclude, on the left, a maximum of three values that are important to you. Then enter, in the other fields, ideas, activities, goals that you would like to bring more of into your life within the next three, six, or twelve months. Keep it joyful and light, this is supposed to nourish your soul.

12 months			
6 months			
3 months			
Value			

OVERVIEW OF EXERCISES

INDEX

ABOUT THE AUTHOR

Photo by Ellen Le Roy

Born in the Bronx (a New York City girl), international author and teacher **Kathryn Hudson** helps people open their channel to Divine guidance, clear communication, and abundance on all levels. Through working with Angels and crystals, and energy in general, Kathryn helps individuals and also groups get into their Flow and fully express their life purpose.

This ex-banker's life changed forever when an Angel walked into a Manhattan bank with a message for her; with this book, she pays that forward. Kathryn has published several books in French, and now in English. Look for her books *Inviting Angels into Your Life* and *Discover Your Crystal Family*, also published by Findhorn Press, if you would like to go deeper into Angelic connection.

Kathryn lives in Paris, France, as well as the Bronx, New York, and Emerald Isle, North Carolina, in the United States. For more information, visit her website: **kathrynhudson.net,** or follow her Daily Messages from the Angels on Instagram or her professional page on Facebook.

Also by Kathryn Hudson

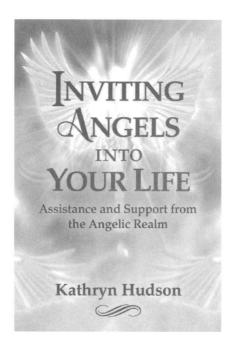

Inviting Angels into Your Life

Assistance and Support from the Angelic Realm

A powerful, step-by-step manual for living joyfully with the
help of the angels, Kathryn Hudson shows how to connect with
15 Archangels and their specific divine qualities. You will learn how
to handle your energy levels in a less than perfect world and maintain
a higher vibration, exploring inner child work, chakra practices, and
exercises for purification and harmonization of relationships. Taking
you from simple questions and requests to direct experience and actual
co-creation with the angelic realm, this guide reveals how to team up
with our friends in high places to open your heart and live out your
highest and best version of yourself in this life.

ISBN 978–1-64411-172-7

Also by Kathryn Hudson

Discover Your Crystal Family

Working with Stones and Their Angelic Messengers

Crystals cross our life path not by accident.
Energetic mirrors of the angelic realm, they allow
us to connect deeply with Heaven and Earth, calling us
in to align with our soul purpose. A natural resonance with
individual Archangels reinforces their particular strengths
and properties, and as we engage with them we can deepen
our energetic health on all levels. Includes a full-color
compendium of 44 crystal allies and their angelic
counterparts, explaining their uses and energies
as well as their spiritual messages.

ISBN 978–1-64411-302-8

FINDHORN PRESS

Life-Changing Books

Learn more about us and our books at
www.findhornpress.com

For information on the Findhorn Foundation:
www.findhorn.org